Blue Remembered Hills

A Recollection

By Rosemary Sutcliff

With an Introduction by Tom Shakespeare

**Handheld
Press**

Handheld Classic 37

This edition published in 2024 by Handheld Press
72 Warminster Road, Bath BA2 6RU, United Kingdom.
www.handheldpress.co.uk

ISBN 978-1-912766-80-2

1 2 3 4 5 6 7 8 9 0

Series design by Nadja Robinson and typeset in Adobe Caslon Pro and Open Sans.

Printed and bound in Great Britain by Short Run Press, Exeter.

Blue Remembered Hills

More Handheld Classics

Henry Bartholomew (ed.), *The Living Stone. Stories of Uncanny Sculpture, 1858–1943*

Betty Bendell, *My Life And I. Confessions of an Unliberated Housewife*, 1966–1980

Algernon Blackwood, *The Unknown. Weird Writings, 1900–1937*

Ernest Bramah, *What Might Have Been. The Story of a Social War* (1907)

D K Broster, *From the Abyss. Weird Fiction, 1907–1940*

John Buchan, *The Gap in the Curtain* (1932)

John Buchan, *The Runagates Club* (1928)

Melissa Edmundson (ed.), *Women's Weird. Strange Stories by Women, 1890–1940*

Melissa Edmundson (ed.), *Women's Weird 2. More Strange Stories by Women, 1891–1937*

Zelda Fitzgerald, *Save Me The Waltz* (1932)

Marjorie Grant, *Latchkey Ladies* (1921)

A P Herbert, *The Voluble Topsy, 1928–1947*

Inez Holden, *Blitz Writing. Night Shift & It Was Different At The Time* (1941 & 1943)

Inez Holden, *There's No Story There. Wartime Writing, 1944–1945*

Margaret Kennedy, *Where Stands A Wingèd Sentry* (1941)

Rose Macaulay, *Non-Combatants and Others. Writings Against War, 1916–1945*

Rose Macaulay, *Personal Pleasures. Essays on Enjoying Life* (1935)

Rose Macaulay, *Potterism. A Tragi-Farcical Tract* (1920)

Rose Macaulay, *What Not. A Prophetic Comedy* (1918)

James Machin (ed.) *British Weird. Selected Short Fiction, 1893–1937*

Vonda N McIntyre, *The Exile Waiting* (1975)

Elinor Mordaunt, *The Villa and The Vortex. Supernatural Stories, 1916–1924*

Jane Oliver and Ann Stafford, *Business as Usual* (1933)

John Llewelyn Rhys, *England Is My Village, and The World Owes Me A Living* (1939 & 1941)

John Llewelyn Rhys, *The Flying Shadow* (1936)

Malcolm Saville, *Jane's Country Year* (1946)

Helen de Guerry Simpson, *The Outcast and The Rite. Stories of Landscape and Fear, 1925–1938*

J Slauerhoff, *Adrift in the Middle Kingdom*, translated by David McKay (1934)

Ann Stafford, *Army Without Banners* (1942)

Amara Thornton and Katy Soar (eds), *Strange Relics. Stories of Archaeology and the Supernatural, 1895–1954*

Elizabeth von Arnim, *The Caravaners* (1909)

Sylvia Townsend Warner, *Kingdoms of Elfin* (1977)

Sylvia Townsend Warner, *Of Cats and Elfins. Short Tales and Fantasies* (1927–1976)

Sylvia Townsend Warner, *T H White. A Biography* (1967)

Contents

The text for this edition was scanned from the 1984 Oxford University Press paperback edition. Typographic errors have been silently corrected. Some terms from the 1980s relating to intellectual and physical difference have not been altered to bring them up to date, since they are the terms that Sutcliff used herself, and accepted in her own environment.

Tom Shakespeare is an English sociologist and bioethicist, and teaches and researches a wide range of issues stemming from disability and bioethics. He is a disability rights campaigner and a broadcaster and has held positions with the World Health Organisation, the Arts Council and Norwich Medical School. His most recent book was *Openings to the Infinite Ocean. A friendly offering of hope* (2020).

Introduction

BY TOM SHAKESPEARE

You are about to read *Blue Remembered Hills*, a lovely memoir by the British novelist Rosemary Sutcliff which is remarkable both for its openness and also because it is one of the very few autobiographies of disabled people available. A few years ago, I read it eager for insights about one of my favourite children's authors. I didn't learn a lot of relevance to her books. Instead, I learned what childhood was like for a clever disabled girl in the 1920s and 30s, and I discovered her, and what made her, in pages that are as vivid as only a true writer could make. Vivid, and also true. For example, when Sutcliff describes unrequited love affairs with people who clearly admired her brains and personality, but did not consider her as a potential life partner, I knew something of how she must have felt, and admired her for surviving these trials. She would have been over-protected and patronised wherever she turned, and yet she became her own person. Luckily, both for my father, born a few years after her, and in turn for me, both born with similarly societally limiting conditions, these difficulties finally gave way to romantic fulfilment. This sort of satisfaction seems to have been absent from Sutcliff's own life; she found her happiness in her writing, her dogs, and her friends.

I first read Rosemary Sutcliff in childhood: at that time, I was keen on reading about historical adventures, and her writing, exploring eras such as Roman Britain and the worlds of the Saxons and Vikings who succeeded them, illuminated exactly the sort of thing I was interested in. Books such as *The Eagle of the Ninth* (1954), *The Shield Ring* (1956) and *The Mark of the Horse Lord* (1965) were among my favourite novels, even though they were published before I was born. Later, I read *The Hobbit* (1937) and C S Lewis's

Narnia stories (1950-56), and then discovered *The Lord of the Rings* (1954-55), and from there moved into the history of Anglo-Saxon England and the Nordic countries, and into the Icelandic sagas. Sutcliff was undoubtedly a gateway for me to the original sources. She brought alive what it might have been like to have lived in those periods better than anyone else. She needed no wardrobe to catapult the reader into another time, nor ring to cast her magic spells.

At Cambridge, I started off studying Anglo-Saxon, Norse and Celtic, turning my hobby into a degree. I moved into Social and Political Sciences for the second part of my degree, and became a sociologist. Ironically, my sociology then took me into disability research, which has been my career ever since. But the fascination with this period of North European history remains. In my fifties, I have returned to Rosemary Sutcliff, reading her as a disabled novelist, because I learned that she lived with juvenile arthritis. Only in my fifties have I finally finished reading the trilogy begun with *The Eagle of the Ninth*. I re-bought these books, as well as other childhood favourites such as *The Shield Ring, Sword Song* (1997) and *The Mark of the Horse Lord*.

Many disabled people have to live emaciated lives: Sutcliff never had a partner or children of her own. But like the Finnish painter Helene Schjerfbeck, another lonely young disabled woman, Sutcliff turned to creativity in order to live fully. When other areas of life are shut off, as they were in earlier centuries for disabled people, and when one yearns to express oneself, the arts are sometimes the sole accessible channel. Sutcliff only went to school at age 9, and left when she was 14; she never went to university. But she was read to as a child by her mother Elizabeth Sutcliff, and from this rich diet of story came the flowering of her vivid imagination, which led in time to more than sixty books, many of which are still read today.

Disability was part of Sutcliff's own life, and perhaps naturally, it was also present in many of her dashing young heroes, such as

Drem, the tribesman with a withered arm in *Warrior Scarlet* (1958). There is congenital impairment in *The Queen Elizabeth Story* (1950, Adam Hilyarde), *Lady in Waiting* (1957, Robert Cecil), *Dawn Wind* (1961, Vadir Cedricson), *Sword at Sunset* (1963, Gwalchmai) and *Song for a Dark Queen* (1978, Claudius). There is acquired physical impairment in *The Chronicles of Robin Hood* (1950, Robin), *Simon* (1953, John Carey), *The Eagle of the Ninth* (1954, Marcus), *Warrior Scarlet* (1958, Talore), *The Mark of the Horse Lord* (1965, Midir), *The Flowers of Adonis* (1969, Timotheus), *The Capricorn Bracelet* (1973, Lucianus Calpurnius), *Blood Feud* (1976, Jestyn Englishman, Hakon One-Eye, Bardas Schlerus) *Shifting Sands* (1977, Moon-Eye), *Bonnie Dundee* (1983, Hugh Herriot), *Blood and Sand* (1987, Anoud bin Aziz ibn Rashid), *The Shining Company* (1990, Conn) and *Sword Song* (1997, Onund Treefoot). Listing them is significant; you realise that Sutcliff created, or chose to accentuate, disabled characters in approximately one third of her books. I cannot think of another writer who has done more or better.

In some ways, a disabled character, set apart from others, is an ideal central character. Impairment is no obstacle to adventure for any of these people. They encounter difficulties, and overcome them. They can still be romantic heroes. They are all real people, not prejudiced stereotypes. Perhaps this normality is because impairment, caused by injury and illness, was common in earlier societies, due to more violence, more poverty, and minimal medicine. But it is surely also because disability was Sutcliff's normality, and therefore she never makes it exceptional. I am sure she herself did not enjoy being cosseted or protected, and so neither do her characters. But they do seek relationships and belonging, which is partly why they are always compelling. Another writer pointed out to me that Sutcliff can never have experienced anything like the cross-country escape described in *The Eagle of the Ninth*, for example, which makes her writing all the more compelling. Denied adventures of her own, she depicted them powerfully in her stories.

Rosemary Sutcliff was born at East Clandon in Surrey in 1920, and died in Walberton, West Sussex in 1992. In her childhood, as described in this memoir, she and her mother followed her father, a Royal Navy officer, in his postings to different Navy dockyards. Sutcliff had juvenile arthritis (Still's Disease), an autoinflammatory condition which causes joint pain, stiffness, and fever, and restricts mobility. In this era it was poorly understood, and she talks of being treated by the physician Sir George Still: he was the first to name the condition, and wrote his dissertation about it. Later he was a physician to the Royal Household, and became known as 'the father of paediatrics' after his death in 1941. In our own day there are more drugs available, including better painkillers, although the condition cannot be cured. In the 1920s there were painful physical treatments, over which Sutcliff largely draws a veil, although she does describe long periods as a resident at the Princess Elizabeth Orthopaedic Hospital in Exeter. This pioneering hospital, built largely with voluntary subscriptions, was opened by the then Duchess of York in 1927, and named after her daughter, later Queen Elizabeth II. The hospital served Devon and parts of Cornwall and Dorset. In the 1940s, Barbara Hepworth did many drawings of operations at the Princess Elizabeth Orthopaedic Hospital while her daughter was treated there, which can still be seen at the Hepworth Gallery at Wakefield. It is well to remember that the word 'orthopaedics' literally means 'child correction'. Reading this memoir, you could imagine how isolated Sutcliff was, stuck on her cold hospital ward, undergoing painful procedures, taking refuge perhaps in her imagination.

Isolation was also a result of being mainly educated at home by her mother, who had what might now be diagnosed as bipolar disorder, which was not always easy to cope with. It was her mother who introduced Sutcliff to the history behind many of the stories she would later write, as well as the work of Rudyard Kipling, who was one of the inspirations for her later fiction. Like Kipling, Sutcliff loved and wrote about Sussex, and imagined past times in that same countryside. However, she began by training as a painter of miniatures at Bideford Art School in Devon, as she describes in *Blue Remembered Hills*. Sutcliff then turned to writing, and, after her first novel was rejected, she was commissioned by Oxford University Press to write a children's version of the Robin Hood stories, published in 1950.

Her father George Sutcliff lived until the 1980s while her mother died in the 1950s. I imagine Sutcliff's pride in demonstrating to both her parents, but particularly her father, what she was capable of in her writing. Literary success was also a way of pushing back against the doctors and others who had seen her as a victim of her disability and felt sorry for her. As shown in this memoir, she did not feel sorry for herself, despite the pain and limitation which she must have experienced.

In her lifetime, she was recognised as one of the best writers for young people. Among other awards, she won the Carnegie Medal for *The Lantern Bearers* (1959); she was appointed OBE in 1975, and CBE in 1992; she became a Fellow of the Royal Society of Literature in 1982. In her life, Sutcliff was far from stiff. Elaine Moss in a *Guardian* obituary describes her as impish, almost irreverent. Sutcliff kept small dogs, which were known to nip visitors. I wish I knew their names: she was good at names.

She wrote 1,800 words a day, and each of her books went through three hand-written drafts. Her stories are realistic, both in the sense that there she almost never introduces magic into her otherwise realistic worlds, and that the times ring true. It is very hard to recreate a world, particularly when it is barely known by historians, let alone by readers. It is not so much recreating as creating from scratch from the scant remains of a past time. Thorough knowledge of the era is needed, but any available books, archeological sites and museums have to be digested and absorbed, never regurgitated or quoted explicitly. It is this implicit naturalism, a realism born of understanding, which is so convincing to the reader, of any age. Penelope Fitzgerald had the trick of it, and so had Hilary Mantel in her Thomas Cromwell trilogy, and so had Sutcliff, with even less to go on than later authors, as modern archaeological finds and insights were not available to her. I think the secret is to know as much as an expert does, and then let on a little. The reader places confidence in the author, because they seem to be omniscient. The little that they mention rings true, because it seems like a selection from so much more, as if they – and by inference you – are really there. However, Sutcliff is always a writer, not a historian, as she said: '… if it does come to the crunch, I will choose a good story over absolute historical accuracy'.

Much of contemporary children's literature is rightly about the difficulties and dilemmas of today. Sutcliff's writing is set centuries, if not millennia, in the past, but the characters' struggles are often familiar. Cutting through almost all of Sutcliff's novels is the poignancy of a dying world, whether of the Iceni tribe of East Anglia, or the Vikings of the Lake District, or the Romans themselves. Empires and ways of life are about to be lost, but ordinary people can discover heroism in themselves. Outsiders change in the process of growing up and conquering against all odds. Continuity is an important element for the reader, as with the engraved emerald signet ring passed on through the series of novels which begins with *The Eagle of the Ninth*. The ending of most of Sutcliff's novels is hopeful, despite this changing world.

There is not much religion: Sutcliff said that she found the Medieval period difficult to write in because of the all-pervasiveness of Christianity having 'a stranglehold on life'. There is a lot of fighting. As she said, 'When the urge to write about a character comes into my mind it never seems to be a peaceful stay-at-home character doing something perfectly worthwhile in a quieter way. It always seems to be a fighting man who appeals to me. I don't know why: I am not a butch character.' There is quite a lot of healing as well, which always fascinated her. Her plots are echoes from medieval minstrels' lays about the once and future king, and in turn produce echoes that can be found in cowboy films, in *Star Wars*, and perhaps in contemporary struggles to save a habitable environment for humanity. The themes are eternal, and therefore timelessly relevant.

It is this heroism in the face of loss which appeals to readers and listeners who are born into a very different world from that which Sutcliff knew, and even more from the times she wrote about. As Margaret Meek says, Rosemary Sutcliff's skills is in 'recreating spots of time when change is both dramatic and threatening'. It is remarkable that one whose life was apparently so static and secure could write about such people and such moments. But then Rosemary Sutcliff became a remarkable person. This book shows where she started from, and what her struggles felt like.

Works by Rosemary Sutcliff

Non-fiction
Houses and History (1960)
Rudyard Kipling (1960)
Heroes and History (1965)
A Saxon Settler (1965)
Blue Remembered Hills: A recollection (1983).

Fiction
The Chronicles of Robin Hood (1950)
The Queen Elizabeth Story (1950)
The Armourer's House (1951)
Brother Dusty-Feet (1952)
Simon (1953)
The Eagle of the Ninth (1954)
Outcast (1955)
The Shield Ring (1956)
The Silver Branch (1957)
Warrior Scarlet (1958)
The Lantern Bearers (1959)
Knight's Fee (1960)
Bridge Builders (1960)
Dawn Wind (1961)
Beowulf: Dragonslayer (1961)
Sword at Sunset (1963)
The Hound of Ulster (1963)
The Mark of the Horse Lord (1965)
The Chief's Daughter (1967)
The High Deeds of Finn MacCool (1967)
A Circlet of Oak Leaves (1968)
The Witch's Brat (1970)
Tristan and Iseult (1971)
The Truce of the Games (1971)

Heather, Oak, and Olive (1972)
The Capricorn Bracelet (1973)
The Changeling (1974)
We Lived in Drumfyvie (1975)
Blood Feud (1976)
Sun Horse, Moon Horse (1977)
Shifting Sands (1977)
Song for a Dark Queen (1978)
The Light Beyond the Forest (1979)
Frontier Wolf (1980)
Eagle's Egg (1981)
The Sword and the Circle (1981)
The Road to Camlann (1981)
Bonnie Dundee (1983)
Flame-Coloured Taffeta (1986)
The Roundabout Horse (1986)
A Little Dog Like You (1987)
The Shining Company (1990)
The Minstrel and the Dragon Pup (1993, posthumous)
Black Ships Before Troy (1993, posthumous)
Chess-Dream in a Garden (1993, posthumous)
The Wanderings of Odysseus (1995, posthumous)
Sword Song (1997, posthumous)

Novels for adults
Lady in Waiting (1957)
The Rider of the White Horse (1959)
The Flowers of Adonis (1969)
Blood and Sand (1987)

This book is for Kathleen Lines

1

When anybody asks me where I was born, or when I am called on to provide that information in filling in a form, I admit with a distinct sense of apology that I was born in Surrey. Why the sense of apology I do not know. Surrey is quite as rich in history and, at least in parts, quite as beautiful in its own way as any other county in England. I can only think that it is because my father, like all the best sailors except Nelson, was Devon born and bred, and my mother was born in Dorset; and because of that, I grew up with the feeling that the West Country is the only right and proper place in which to have one's beginnings.

I come of a dynasty of doctors on both sides, with a scattering of farmers and merchants — the latter mostly Quakers and, on my father's side, one colourful character who began life in the Navy, was wounded at Waterloo, having changed over into the Army meanwhile, and ended up as governor of some West Indian colony. On my mother's side the medical tradition ended with her father. All her brothers went to the Engineering College at Coopers Hill and thence to India; the old India of the Raj, almost of Kipling, to spend most of their working lives building railways and the like. My father's brothers and two of his brothers-in-law were all doctors, and he always claimed that his original reason for going into the Navy like his predecessor of Waterloo fame was a strong objection to following through Epsom and St Thomas's the footsteps of too many relations who had all done a good deal better there than he was likely to do himself. My father had no great opinion of his own mental abilities, and on the principle that the fool of the family goes to sea, departed seaward at the age of thirteen, entering the Navy via the

Conway instead of Dartmouth, because his Latin was not up to the Dartmouth standard. However, as the *Conway* was primarily a training ship for the Merchant Service, and only a small proportion of its boys, John Masefield among them, ever made the Royal Navy, and as he did manage to pass out top of his term, with the King's binoculars to show for it, he cannot have been so very dim, after all.

He was a lieutenant when he and my mother were married. They had first met when they were both fourteen, at a mixed hockey match, and he always claimed that the first word he ever heard her say was 'Damn', which I suppose, to judge from her vehemence in protesting that it was the first time she had ever said it, was quite a word in those days. My father's invariable retort — oh, the lovely ritual changelessness of family jokes and traditions! — was that for a first time, she said it with remarkable fluency.

My father's elder sister was married to a bank manager in Poole, where my mother's father had his practice, and from the time of the hockey match he took to spending as much as possible of his leaves with her, between long absences at sea. In those days a naval officer was at sea as a midshipman by the age of sixteen, and from then on, single or married, was frequently away from his nearest and dearest for two solid years at a time, with no means of contact save by letter.

Three days after their wedding he went off to South Africa for three years, while she remained in England to look after her mother, who was an invalid suffering from rheumatoid arthritis, and by then a widow. He had not long been home again when the First World War broke out, so that was another four years before they got around to having a baby at all. Then came Penelope, who died when only a few months old, in the terrible post-war 'flu epidemic. A few more years, and I was born. My father was at the Admiralty at the time, and commuting daily between Whitehall and

East Clandon, which is how just before Christmas 1920 I came to be born in Surrey.

For some years, I thought that I could remember being born. Later, I realised that I only remembered what I had been told about being born — by my mother, who was of the stuff that minstrels are made, but singularly unaware of the effect that her stories might have on a small daughter who believed implicitly in every word she uttered. So then, my birth-memory, via my mother, was of being brought by the stork in the middle of a desperate snowstorm. I was really intended for Mrs McPhee who lived next door, and who had, said my mother, made ready whole drawers full of baby-clothes including tiny kilts, and decided to call me Jeannie; but in the appalling snow he lost his way and came knocking on our door, begging to be taken in for the night, failing which he would have to go to the police, and I would be put in an orphanage. It was a very bad storm, and my teeth were chattering; so my mother took pity on us and let us come in and sit by the fire and gave us both hot cocoa, after which the stork departed, leaving me behind and promising to come back for me next day. He never came, and so there I still was, with Mummy and Daddy, two or three years later. I was a trusting child, or possibly just plain gullible. I never thought to wonder why, if the story were true, I had not merely been handed over the garden fence to my rightful owners next morning. Nor did it occur to me that at age zero, I would have been unlikely to have teeth to chatter.

It was a grief to me that I did not truly belong to my parents, but presumably I was unable to make this known; and when I was nearly four, and somebody said to me, in my mother's presence, 'What's your name, little girl?' to which I replied in a voice quivering with emotion, 'I'm really little Jeannie McPhee, but I'm living with Daddy and Mummy just now,' my mother was the world's most surprised and horrified woman. But she never learned.

Though that particular account of my birth was apocryphal, there seem to have been quite a few genuine dramas attached to the event. The doctor said I was due to arrive on Christmas Eve; my mother said I was coming on December 14th, and on the 14th I came. Having a kind of two-thirds belief in horoscopes, I have sometimes wondered what effect that has had on my life and on the kind of person I am. I was born in a blizzard, and we had run out of coal and my father had to go next door, presumably to the McPhees, to borrow some in a wheelbarrow; and when next day the coalman did arrive, his horse fell down under the bedroom window.

I don't, then, actually remember being born; but I do have a genuine first memory that goes back to the time when I was eighteen months old. We were staying with my dear Uncle Harold, whose home, when he was not in India, was still at Poole in Dorset; and my mother had me out in my pram in Poole Park. We came trundling along a path between big dark evergreen bushes reaching to the sky. The path turned a corner, and the bushes fell back forming a small open space in which were wire-netting cages containing large birds which look in my memory like golden pheasants. I did not so much mind the pheasants, but there was another cage holding captive a restless revolving red squirrel, at sight of which all the woes of the world, all sins and sorrows, all injustice, all man's inhumanity to man came crashing in one great engulfing wave over my eighteen-month-old head, which was not yet ready to cope with it. I took one look, and broke into a roar of grief and fury which nothing would console or quieten, until I had been smartly trundled out of the gardens.

Afterwards we both forgot about the whole thing until

after I was grown up, when something, I have no idea what, triggered the old memory, and back came the pictures. I described the incident to my mother. Had it ever happened, or was I inventing it? My mother thought — and remembered also; all too vividly. It had been dreadful, she said. I had gone on and on, and she hadn't even been able to slap me because she had actually agreed with me entirely, and her mother, my grandmother, had hated things in cages so much that she had vowed to vote for any government that would abolish menageries and travelling circuses; and my face had been purple, and it had taken the gift of a green balloon to silence me at last; and I knew how much she disapproved of bribery. She added that I couldn't have been more than eighteen months old because after that we were never in Poole Park again until I was seven.

Which is how I know that, unlike the stork saga, it was a genuine memory.

It is, in fact, my only memory of the time before I contracted juvenile arthritis. Because my next memory, which must date from a year later, is of being ill in bed with pains in my joints, and being visited by an aged relative, who, so far as I know, I never saw before or after, called Auntie Katie. This memory is connected with biscuits and doll's furniture. Either I was eating biscuits and she brought me a present of doll's furniture, or I was playing with doll's furniture and she brought me biscuits.

The other thing I remember about the earlier and more active stages of my illness is having a black panther under my bed. After a while it was discovered that I was simply hallucinating as the result of too much arsenic in the medicine I was being given; but at the time it must have been even more terrifying for my parents than it was for me. Always at night it came on; first the black panther under my bed, then wolves crowding in the shadowy corners of the room out of range of the nightlight, then snakes climbing up the walls. And my mother, finding that nothing else would reassure me, would spend large parts of each night carrying me wrapped in a shawl round and round the room and into all the corners, making me pat the walls to show myself that there was nothing there.

The strange thing was that I had of course never seen a black panther, nor a wolf, nor a snake; and yet, remembering what I saw, they were wolves skulking in the corners, not fantasy creatures. And years later when I met Kipling's *Jungle Books*, I recognised them; and strangest of all, recognised them not with fear, but with love. Bagheera, the black panther with a voice as soft as wild honey dripping from a tree, was one of the deepest loves of my childhood, and to this day very few fictional characters have ever come as near to my heart. So why was I frightened at our first meeting? Maybe I caught my poor mother's fear. I do not know. It is all very odd.

2

When I was not much past three years old, my father was ordered to join the *Benbow* of the Mediterranean Fleet, and it was decided that heat might be good for whatever it was that was wrong with me — not even Dr Still, whose special study it was, seemed to know much about juvenile arthritis in those days, save that it was a form of acute arthritis that attacked children, bringing with it waves of acute pain and fever with joint inflammation, that came and went with periods of remission in between for an indefinite number of years, and eventually, if it did not kill one first, burned itself out, leaving havoc behind it. They still weren't even sure if that was what I had. And so my mother and I went out to Malta, where the Fleet was based, and naval wives and families congregated.

To this day the name 'Malta' means bells to me. Bells ringing, not as the church bells ring in this country, but clashing all together, tossing and falling and fountaining above the roof-tops and through the narrow streets, And I see the blue of a night sky through a mosquito net; and somehow superimposed on that, the top of an orange-tree triumphant with flaming golden fruit peering at me over the broken coping of a sunlit wall.

It isn't, I suppose, surprising that my memories of Malta should be only a series of small unconnected pictures, because I was still only somewhere between four and five when we came home again. Perhaps 'unconnected' is not quite the right word, for the pictures do form a kind of pattern in my mind; a mosaic made up of small brilliantly-coloured pieces laced together with the bright filigree of the bells.

At the centre of it all was our house in Sliema, rented

furnished from two very great and gracious ladies, who refused, at the end of our time there, to have the inventory checked, saying that they should not dream of so insulting my mother. The outside of the house is gone from me, but the inside was grey; a greenish underwater grey filled with shadows and coolness; with quiet, tall, immensely dignified rooms whose stone floors were washed daily with paraffin in the water to discourage the ants and other creepy-crawlies. They were washed by our maid Lucille Azzipadi, who I remember for one dramatic pronouncement, made with flashing eyes and hands on hips, in some time of strife at home: 'My fader, he debbil man!'

The walls of our house were lined with portraits of cardinals and archbishops, all relatives of the two great ladies through many generations. Their eyes used to follow us through the day; eyes out of dark subtle faces under cardinals' hats, resting on us wherever we went, whatever we did, until my mother turned them all round with their faces to the walls, and we lived quite happily thereafter with their brownish canvas backs.

Unfortunately it was not possible to turn round in the same way the windows of our dining-room, which looked directly into the street, and through which, consequently, the street looked directly into our dining-room. When too many Maltese urchin noses became glued to the glass, the grown-ups within cried, 'Impshi!' with no appreciable result. When the concentration of noses became unbearable, the grown-ups cried 'Impshi Gehenna!' which got instant results, but had such a blighting effect, scattering the urchin noses as from actual danger, that neither my mother nor my father had the heart to use it unless and until driven to frenzy.

I remember our garden, so tiny and so high-walled that it was like a room roofed with blue sky, a garden paved for the most part, and with three steps leading down into it. I am sure that there were three, because I remember sitting exactly halfway down, with one step behind me and one step still to go, watching the spread-fingered lizards darting among the cracks in the warm stones. And just space in it for a well, a frangipani climbing over one wall and a lemon tree.

In the mornings our garden was cool in shadow, and Mrs Paterson from across the street, who I was told expected the stork to bring her a baby quite soon, would bring her needlework and come and sit with us on the steps, while the strip of shade grew slowly narrower, and the sunshine crept towards us like a bright blasting curtain. In the afternoon, when our garden had become an oven in which the heat danced like a swarm of midges, and the shade had all gone across the street, we went across the street too, and sat on the steps in Mrs Paterson's garden. But I do not remember whether she had a well or a frangipani or a lemon tree.

There is the centre of the mosaic, and the rest falls into place around it.

I remember a road clouded with dust, which I thought led right across the island in one ruled line, and which seemed to me, though I do not think this can really have been so, just as I do not think I can really have seen respectable Presbyterian Mrs Paterson sitting up in bed in a black satin nightdress, to be bordered as far as the eye could see, therefore all the way, with stone jars of some blue flower with a hairy stem.

I remember the streets being full of priests and goats in about equal quantities, the priests, though this also on reflection seems unlikely, with the ends of white crochet lace petticoats showing under their cassocks. The Fleet used to play a game called Priests, derived from the better-known game of Beaver. Two men would take opposite sides of a street and count priests instead of beards. It was a more complex game than Beaver because the different grades of churchmen rated different points; one for a parish priest, two for a tonsured monk, and so on, right up to the Archbishop. If you met him you won the game outright. The two players would progress along the street calling out the score to each other as they went. But, alas, the Church did not appreciate their innocent pastime, and in the end the game was officially outlawed.

The goats were led from door to door to be milked into jugs which the women brought out for the purpose, or merely wandered unattended with no obvious aim in view; old mangy billies, gaunt nannies with their kids at heel, and generally a rotten cabbage leaf or a half-eaten paper bag hanging from their mouths. The children of the garrison and the lean pale-grey warships in the Grand Harbour never drank goats' milk, for it carried the Malta fever, and since there were no cows on the island, another of my memories, less pleasant than some, is of condensed milk, well laced with tea to disguise the horrible taste, which somehow it never did.

Of the Maltese goats, or of one in particular, I have one really shattering memory. My mother, still not realising how implicitly I believed her lightest word, once told me that if I did that again, whatever that was, the Black Goat would come and eat me. Shortly afterwards she left me parked in my pushchair outside a shop for a few minutes while she went in; whereupon, up the street came a whole flock of goats in every stage of dilapidation, and of every colour including black. My mother, recalled by my terrified shrieks, came flying out to find me hanging by a hair from my pushchair on one side, while a kindly old black billy with his forehooves inside it on the other, nibbled at me with an air of vaguely wondering what all the uproar was about. Maybe he had mistaken me for a particularly succulent paper bag, though it is much more likely that he only wished to be friendly. But at the time I certainly thought that not only death but damnation was upon me.

Goats were not the only carriers of illness; there was the sandfly. But against sandfly fever one could be inoculated, and I have another, hideously vivid picture of a great menacing brute of a doctor sticking a Thing that ended in a vicious needle into my mother's arm. Mad to defend my own, I scrambled off my father's knee, and flew to her rescue. I fixed my teeth in the doctor's horrible hairy wrist and hung on like a terrier, until my father succeeded in prising me away. Afterwards, everybody said how wonderful the doctor had been, because he continued calmly giving the inoculation while I was prised off him, instead of breaking the needle in my mother's arm. But nobody said how brave it was of me, only three years old, when all is said and done, and gone in the legs at that, to take on such fearful odds for the sake of love.

There were nannies in Malta; aproned nannies, who had no surnames of their own, but were known by those of the families they were attached to. Nannie Kendle, who was starchy and Scottish and kept Patsy crackling with cleanliness, and crowned as it were with the splendour of lace on her drawers! Patsy was the only child of my acquaintance to have lace on her drawers, for children's underwear was for the most part depressingly plain and serviceable in the days when I wore it. Nannie Domville, large and bosomy, whose charge was slightly 'odd' (he grew up, I believe, to be a perfectly normal pillar of society) and who attributed this to the fact that he had been taken as a toddler to see his grandfather in Court dress complete with sword and cocked hat. And what sight was that, Nannie Domville demanded indignantly of my mother, for any sensitive child? As the grandfather was generally spoken of by his friends and well-wishers the length and breadth of the Navy as Monkey Domville for painfully obvious reasons, and Baby Domville had taken one look at him, screamed wildly and fallen in a fit, I do feel that she had a point.

All my friends had nannies, which shows how much the world has changed in half a century; for we were the children of very ordinary naval and army officers with nothing but their pay. But I never had a nannie of my own. That was because I was still being ill — ill in patches and better in patches, and sometimes very ill indeed, as the arthritis burned its way along, and attack and remission followed each other during all the time that we were in Malta. My mother would not trust me to another woman's care.

How I wished sometimes in later years that she had!

My mother was one of those people, generally, I think, women, capable of great love and great self-sacrifice, but not capable of giving these things without demanding a return. During those years, she devoted herself to me to an extent which I sometimes think must have come hard on my father. She was not really beautiful, certainly not pretty, but she had one of those enchanting, changeable faces that can put on beauty, and lose it, and find it again as quickly as the changing lights of a March day; and a mass of golden hair. A young man had called her 'Golden-haired Nerissa', on board ship going to India, and written a poem to her. She had been outrageously spoiled as a girl, with every young man in sight trailing after her. She loved dancing and parties, and for my sake she missed almost all the social life of the Mediterranean station. What that must have meant to her, quite apart from the heartbreak of any mother coping with a sick child who was more than once in acute danger and rapidly becoming a handicapped child, is painful even to think of.

She was wonderful, no mother could have been more

wonderful. But ever after, she demanded that I should not forget it, nor cease to be grateful, nor hold an opinion different from her own, nor even, as I grew older, feel the need for any companionship but hers. If this seems a terrible thing to write, I can argue only that it is the truth, and if I left it comfortably unwritten, I could not give a true picture of our relationship, which was a very close one, almost as close at times as she thought it was, and as she would have liked it to be. But it was never, after the very early years, an easy one. Very few of the worthwhile things in this world are all that easy.

So — l had no nannie, and because of that, we shared our Malta far more closely than did most mothers and children.

Of the illness which brought that about, I remember chiefly the nights; the long hot nights when it seemed that the sirocco was always blowing, and yet there was never enough air inside the mosquito net; and my mother sitting up with me and telling me stories. These generally had their origin in the Old Testament, but had come a long way since. There was one in particular, about how Miss Lot failed to catch the Ark when the Flood came, because she was too busy enjoying herself at a teaparty, and was turned into a pillar of salt as a punishment. 'And that,' said my mother, 'is why the sea is salt. It is Miss Lot down at the bottom, still melting.'

To those nights also belongs the small, infinitely clear memory of the colour of a night sky seen through a mosquito net, when there is a small light in the bedroom, a wonderfully gentle blue, a little like the colour of wild hyacinths in a wood, but not quite. It is not quite like anything that I have seen since.

I wish that I could truthfully fit some pictures of the Fleet at anchor in the Grand Harbour under the bastions of Valetta into my mosaic, because I must have seen it so often, and I feel that it should by rights be there. But, alas, it is not, and there is no help for it. And the only memory I have even of the *Benbow*, or the *Iron Duke* to which my father was transferred after the first few months, is of a children's party on board; and the only thing I remember with any clearness about that is the crystallised orange and lemon slices, of which, so far as possible, I made my tea.

It was in Malta that my mother and I had our first full-blown battle of wills. It concerned the direction we should take for an afternoon walk. (I suppose that we did not, after all, spend every afternoon in Mrs Paterson's garden.) My mother's choice was St Julien's Bay, where there was nothing but sea and rocks and solitude, and if one could not wander off among the rock pools to annoy the sea anemones, as I could not, nothing to do but sit on the rocks and watch the sea and feel the solitude breathing down the back of one's neck. I wanted to go along the harbour front. It had a proper name, but since it was in Arabic, I have not the remotest idea how to write it down. It sounded like Ghara Dut. Here there would be dogs barking and beggars begging, and crowds and peculiar smells, and Life going on with a capital L in all directions. My mother went on and on towards St Julien's Bay, and I in my pushchair abandoned myself to earsplitting grief and disappointment. Half-way there, feeling I suppose that her eardrums or her reason would stand the strain no longer, she stopped in her tracks, and put two alternatives to me. She said, 'Either we will go quietly to St Julien's Bay and spend the afternoon there, and have chocolate biscuits for tea when we get home again, or we will go home now and I shall give you a hard smacking, and then we will go along the Ghara Dut.'

The offer seemed to me a fair one, and I chose the smacking and the Ghara Dut.

We went home in frozen silence, and in the cool grey

dignity of our hall, the cardinals and bishops with their backs turned, I was upended and received the hard smacking promised me. My mother was efficient in the administering of corporal punishment, though she did not do it very often, and I always felt for half an hour afterwards as though I was sitting on a hot-water bottle. Punishment over, I said between hiccups, 'And now us go along Ghara Dut.'

My mother was a woman of her word, and along the Ghara Dut we went.

In after years we tried more than once to decide which of us had had the victory in that encounter, but could never make up our minds,

For the rest — I remember so many things of those Malta years. The taste of blood-oranges still warm from the tree. A piece of pumice-stone I loved, which was stolen from me by a wicked boy. The string of amber which my father brought me back from Istanbul, still generally called Constantinople in those days, made of odd beads from broken-up Mohammedan rosaries, smoky-coloured from the nicotine-stained fingers of the Faithful telling over the ninety and nine names of Allah. (Only the camel knows the hundredth, and that is why he looks so supercilious.)

I suppose it is because he was so often away with the Fleet, returning briefly from magic-sounding places such as Egypt and Constantinople, the Greek Islands or the Holy Land, only to disappear again before I had even got used to him being at home, that I remember so little of my father during that time. I remember far better the brother and sister who looked after the officers' bathing pool, both of them with sea-blue eyes, and hair bleached pale as driftwood by the sun and salt, and a kind of harsh and strenuous beauty about them that I recognised even then. And I remember a boyfriend I had, who believed in caveman tactics and used to hit me over the head with the nearest blunt instrument, generally a wooden spade, whenever we met, by way of showing his affection; and who, when the time came for parting, a time which comes so soon and so often to service children, cast himself upon my distinctly unresponsive stomach, wailing, 'Oh, Honey-bun, Honey-bun! Say you won't forget your Henery Cox!'

And I never have. Though truth to tell, my own best-beloved while we were in Malta was a red-headed sick-bay steward, who used to come up three times a week to give me massage and exercise — physiotherapy, I suppose it would be called now. Him I loved most dearly and deeply, even when he hurt me. His name was O'Brien, but to me he was always 'Mr O'Browne, *dear* Mr O'Browne.'

But the time had come for parting from him also. The time for going home to England. I wept on his neck; and he was nicer to me in my grief that I fear I was to Henery Cox. I have never seen nor heard of either of them again from that day to this.

3

Our return journey from Malta came at a time when the whole of Europe was convulsed by some very special event in the Roman Catholic world; and with pressure of pilgrims, all forms of transport had gone mad. The sea voyage to Marseilles was accomplished in an aged ferry steamer whose normal run was only the short haul between Malta and Syracuse, and whose captain was a White Russian princeling of the bluest blood but only minimal knowledge of seamanship. The weather was appalling; the *Lublyana* had every vice known to ships. She not only bounced like a cork and rolled like a farrowing sow, she also corkscrewed. My mother lay on her bunk and hoped audibly that we were going to sink. I was not much affected, and in fact won golden opinions from my father by making a hearty lunch of roast pork in the middle of it all. I can only think that I was a much better sailor then than I am now.

In the vile weather and the unaccustomed seaways, the White Russian prince mislaid Marseilles altogether, and finally, answering calls for professional help from the bridge, my father brought the *Lublyana* into harbour himself.

There must have been a train after that; but the next thing I remember is being in Streatham, Number 66, Norfolk House Road, staying with my Aunt Janet, my father's Scottish eldest sister-in-law, whose husband, like his other brother, had died in the war. She was, as she remained all her life, a very pretty woman, with soft hair and bright blue eyes and a velvety blush-rose skin; and the invincible belief in the superiority of all things Scottish over all things English, which I have since noticed as one of the less endearing traits of quite a few Scots who have elected to live out their lives in England.

It must have been late autumn or early winter, because the trees on Tooting Bec Common, where my mother took me most afternoons, were bare, and blotted with old rooks' nests. And in the wild bit in the heart of the Common, the Dell, I believe it was called, everything was grey and sparkling with the first frost, so far as I know, that I had ever seen. The bramble leaves had ermine edgings which gave off a delicious sensation of prickly cold between my fingers, but rather disappointingly disappeared at the same time, like Fairy Gold. And one afternoon my mother produced a needle and stout black cotton from her handbag, and gathered and strung me an enchanted fiery necklace of coppery haws and scarlet hips.

At 66, Norfolk House Road I had my first experience of wireless, my initiation into the joys of *Children's Hour*. In the dining-room there was a large black box covered with white dials like staring eyes, the property of my cousins, who were already on the edge of being grown up. And one afternoon, the lights on and the curtains drawn for tea, I was sat down in front of it, and a pair of earphones fitted over my head. A man's voice spoke from the earphones directly into my head. It was telling a story. After the first moment of surprise, I sat enthralled. The story is for the most part lost to me, but I do remember that it concerned the adventures of some elves, and that at one point one of the elves had the misfortune to slide down the handle of a silver ladle into a soup tureen. He said, 'Where am I?' and 'they' said, 'You're in the soup!' This, the first joke that ever I remember, struck me as being so exquisitely funny that I rolled about and came perilously near to wetting my knickers.

Next day, my cousins said would I like to listen to *Children's Hour* again. I was enchanted. Like most children, there was nothing I liked better than the same story over and over again. Once more, I sat before the black box with the staring white eyes, the earphones were fitted over my head, and I prepared to be convulsed again by the story of the elf being in the soup. Alas, the voice that came out of the earphones was a different voice, telling a different story, about someone called Robin Hood, whom I had not at that time met. It was one of the great disappointments of my childhood.

For a short while, weeks or months, 'Home' was a cottage we rented near Sevenoaks, and my father was again at the Admiralty and coming back from London each evening. One evening he brought me the nucleus of what was to become a well-stocked toy farm: two cows, one black-and-white lying down, one brown-and-white standing up, and a hen sitting on a nestful of yellow chicks. They were stout heavy little creatures of painted lead. Oh, the satisfying weight and density of the farm animals and toy soldiers of my youth, compared with the flimsy plastic variety with which the modern child has to be content, finely modelled but so light that they blow over if you breathe in their direction. I have always been sorry for children born more than two hundred years ago, and therefore denied the pleasure of popping fuchsia buds, and for children born too late to enjoy, except possibly as family treasures and collector's pieces, the feel of strength and balance and solidity of lead cows or Grenadiers that were a delight to the hand as well as the eye.

And then when I was five we went to Sheerness Dockyard.

4

At Sheerness we lived in one of the lovely dignified Adam houses of Dockyard Terrace.

Going back many years later, after Sheerness had ceased to be a Royal Dockyard, I found that it was a short cosy terrace, and the houses quite small. But at five, it seemed to me that the terrace was a mile long, and the houses reached up to touch the sky. In front of the terrace was a wide green space, with walnut trees standing thoughtfully around on the part that was not given over to tennis courts. There were walnut trees here and there all over the dockyard, and at the proper season the walnuts were picked by the authorities and allocated according to rank, so many basketfuls to the Admiral of the Yard, so many to the Captain, so many to the King's Harbour Master — that was us — to the Chaplain, the Senior Constructor, the Surgeon Commander ...

Behind the terrace were the gardens, high-walled, as our Malta garden had been, but many times larger, with one gardener between them all: Mr Ransome, brown and stooping, like something out of *The Secret Garden* but less agreeable. My father looked after the lawn, spending long summer evenings sitting on it digging out daisies with a broken dinner-knife, and generally lavishing himself upon it until it really was like velvet. Old Ransome looked after the flowers and fruit — big scarlet tulips, I remember, with indigo stars in their hearts when you looked deep down into them; and forget-me-nots growing round their feet; and London Pride. And wall-trained fruit like whiteheart cherries that I ate with brown bread-and-butter, sitting on the back doorstep, for my tea.

Most of my time, when not being taken for afternoon walks in my pushchair — I could not at that time actually walk at all — was spent in the garden or parked under the walnut trees in front; for I was supposed to be out of doors as much as possible. Being out of doors, no matter how wet or cold one got in the process, was supposed to be good for practically everything at that time. But my memories of Sheerness are chiefly spring and summer ones.

I think the arthritis, otherwise known as Still's Disease, must have burned itself out by the time we left Malta, because I have no recollection of being ill in Sheerness, only of having various unsatisfactory joints, and not being able to walk, and going up to London every six weeks to visit a surgeon called Mr Openshaw.

Mr Openshaw, as his name suggests, was a North Countryman, a short tubby man with hands like a butcher's. It is disappointing how few surgeons have the kind of hands one would expect; lean and strong, with waisting between the joints and spatulate finger-tips. In fact, in a fairly wide experience, I think I have only met one who came up to expectations in that respect. Mr Openshaw used to stand with his behind his back, and his head tipped down, staring at one over the top of his gold-rimmed spectacles. He belonged to a school which I suppose is now extinct in this age of technical improvement, and I remember him cutting off a plaster-cast of mine with a thing like a jack-knife. He began at the top, almost at the hip, and ended at the toes, in one steady unceasing cut. I saw with interest his wrist quivering with the force he used. I felt the cold tip of the knife touching me the whole way; but when the cast was broken open and forced off, there was not a scratch, not the faintest mark on my skin.

I was fond of Mr Openshaw, and did not mind the visits at all, though they entailed splints and plaster-casts intended to rest damaged joints and straighten crooked ones, and sometimes he hurt me quite a lot. But though I enjoyed going past the Crystal Palace and Wormwood Scrubs, I did not really like London at that time, and was always glad when the family car — a bull-nosed Morris — was heading the other way. Most of all the homeward journey I enjoyed the first moment of return to Sheerness Marshes; the wide skies, the smell of open space and saltings and clean air, the stray skeins of wild duck overhead. Sheerness Marshes are bleak and hard; but I loved them, and have loved all marsh country for their sake ever since.

When we first arrived at Sheerness Dockyard, my father joined a shooting syndicate and, duty permitting, used to depart at all kinds of ungodly hours, to catch the dawn or evening flight of duck. And that was how Don became a member of our household. We had had a dog, a border collie born by some mischance into a litter of fox-terriers, in pre-Malta days, but though I knew from family legend that his beauty, intelligence and valour were unsurpassed and unsurpassable, I had no memory of him, so Don is really the first dog in my life.

He was a black wavy-coated retriever, and belonged to the shoot. He lived out on the marshes, in the care of a shepherd who seems to have been a disgrace to his kind. Don lived in an old barrel for a kennel, and never had a square meal except when a sheep died. He had lived all his short life — he was only about two years old — without love and without hope; and his disposition had remained as sweet as an apple.

My father and he took one look at each other, and my father said, 'That dog will die if he stays out here much longer. He's coming home with me.'

The rest of the syndicate pointed out that he belonged to the shoot as a whole. The Commander could have him for five pounds.

The Commander said, 'Five pounds be damned! Either

that dog comes home with me, or I go straight to the RSPCA.'

He returned home with Don in the back of the car, black furry chin resting on Harris-tweed shoulder.

They continued — it must have been a tricky situation — to go shooting with the syndicate. But thenceforth Don was our dog and we were his beloved family. My father was his god. When my father was at home, Don lay at his feet, limpid eyes fixed on his face, and every time his god got up, to go down the garden, to the bathroom, or even just across the room to change a record on the wind-up gramophone, Don got up and padded after him. During the daytime, when my father had gone away past the gorgeous painted figureheads that lined the way to his office in the bowels of the dockyard, Don lent his allegiance to me. I was not his god, but I was his godlet; he lay by my pushchair on the terrace, walked between me and the world when we went out in the afternoon; let me, on one occasion, hack chunks out of his beautiful coat with a table-knife. Only once did any disharmony arise between us, and that was when I began to walk again. Don had only seen me, as it were, moving on wheels; and that was obviously the proper way for his godlet to move. The first time he saw me on my feet, he backed away from me growling, bewildered and upset; and it was several days before he could bring himself to accept the change, forgive me for the shock to his system, and talk to me again.

Don was very beautiful, except for his back legs. Malnutrition when he was growing had resulted in something like rickets. In walking, his back legs splayed out sideways in a manner not unlike Charlie Chaplin's; and when he went out shopping with my mother and me the rude little boys of the town used to waddle along like ducklings behind him with shrieks of unseemly laughter.

Don was no fighter, but he would fight when pushed far enough, and when he did, he was dangerous with the danger of a quiet man roused to fury. Only twice during our years together, he fought another dog. Once it was the dockyard bully, an Airedale from further along the terrace who made his life a misery, and whom he bore with for weeks, before finally rounding on him and beating him to a jelly. Once it was a dog of the town, who forced a quarrel on him and got thrashed for his pains. Of that occasion I remember chiefly Don being taken into Smith's, the sweetie shop much beloved by me because it was there that occasionally my mother bought me peppermint creams as a special treat, and having the red juicy holes in his nose bathed by Miss Smith, while everybody told him what a good brave boy he was.

As a result of not being actively ill any longer, though the after-effects of course remained, I soon had a part-time nannie, who came in by the half day. Her name was Ivy, and she had a squint and a black Spanish hat with a red rose under the brim. Both these things fascinated me; the squint because I could never be sure where she was looking, the hat because I thought it was the most beautiful hat I had ever seen.

Another result of my not being ill was that my mother now had much more social life. When she came to say goodnight to me in all her glory before going out to dinner, she would be wearing a dress, short-skirted and with its waist round her hips, of pink and gold brocade; or one which I liked even better — almost as much as Ivy's hat — which was black, held up by a narrow black ribbon over one shoulder and a string of coral beads over the other, and flashing a broad pleat lined with coral pink in the skirt, that appeared and disappeared as she moved. I could draw that dress now.

When she was giving a dinner party instead of going to

one, the crystallised cherries came out, for decorating the trifle, and I used to be given one, just one. What delight, what splendour there was in the soft rich sweetness of that one crystallised cherry! But there was even more, in the tin they came from, a disused Sharpe's Toffee tin, its lid depicting a carnival scene, with masked Harlequin and frilly Columbine against a sky of deepest midnight blue shimmering with lanterns and streamers, in all the colours of a rainbow run mad. I suppose it was all mixed up in my mind with the knowledge that there was going to be a party downstairs after I was in bed, and snatches of voices and laughter that came and went as doors opened and shut, and the mystery that a grown-up party has when one is five years old and supposed to be already asleep. But that tin was one of the magical things of my childhood. They don't make tins like that in these degenerate days.

Myself, I had scarcely any social life at all. That was nobody's fault. It was just that there were no other children of my age in the dockyard. I had almost said of my generation. There was Georgie Goebel, the doctor's son, but he was only three, and an enemy of society anyway; and apart from him, there were shoals of children in the yard, but all in the twelve-to-fourteen age group, and to twelve-to-fourteen, five-to-six is another generation. During term-time they disappeared, but come the holidays, back they all flocked like starlings; and then my father became the most popular man in the yard, for as King's Harbour Master he had his own boat complete with coxswain and crew, which spent much of its time on standby. He had also a good understanding of the tastes of children. So he would gather all the young of dockyard and barracks and send them off on river trips with no grown-ups except Gilson and his merry men — and there is a natural affinity between sailors and children, anyway — and they would explore the coastal inlets and board the brown-sailed Medway barges and picnic on board, and do all manner of exciting and delightful things which Gilson, my friend, would tell me about afterwards. At other times there would be land picnics, several cars, including our bull-nosed Morris, banding together, and crawling off, laden to the gunwales with children sitting on the down-folded roofs and clinging to the running-boards. And I was left behind in my five-year-old world, with Ivy.

I did not really feel bad about it. Looking back, I realise now what I did not realise then — small children accept short-comings in their own bodies with a curious kind of unawareness or only half awareness — that even if I had been their age I would still have been left behind, or else taken and left with the grown-ups when we got there. As it was, I took it quite as a matter of course that they were 'Big' and I was 'Little' and we inhabited different worlds. But I watched them depart with a touch of envy and a wish that I was 'Big' none the less; particularly as I did not really see eye to eye with Ivy in any sense, despite her beautiful hat.

She was not a very understanding person.

Once, the fat sergeant of police on the main gate, who was rather a friend of mine, picked and presented to me an illicit iris from the big round bed just inside the gates. It was a huge and wonderful iris of purple velvet, dark and rich, and with a throat that seemed to reach down into the heart of the world; and I loved it with a great and intense love that took no account of some tiny black things that were walking round the base of the petals. The purple sails of the standards were cool against my face. I felt the silken touch of the falls over my fingers as I gazed down into it ... But as soon as we were out of sight of the gates, Ivy took it off me, saying, 'You don't want that nasty dirty flower, those little black flies will crawl up your nose,' and threw it away.

Actually there must have been other children of around my own age, attached, as it were, to the Senior Officers' School, because I do remember going to the occasional party. The children are faceless; they came from outside the dockyard, and at five, one does not have much of a circle of friends unless they live close by. But I remember the parties, of two kinds. Winter parties, fancy dress, at which everyone arrived wrapped in Shetland shawls like large cocoons, to be unwound by mothers or nannies, revealing the butterfly inside. A fairy, a toy soldier, a pirate ... I had a blue-and-white pierrot suit with a black ruffle that pricked my neck. The very thought of it makes me want to rub the place even now; and the grown-ups never properly understood why I made such a fuss about having that vile pierrot suit put on. Far superior, to my way of thinking, were the summer parties, given by the Crookendens, and held, weather permitting — and as far as I remember, weather always did permit — in the garden of their big Georgian house. Colonel Crookenden was Colonel of the Senior Officers' School, and the house, like ours, went with the job. The Crookendens never went in for organised party games or prizes, or a conjuror. They merely provided a splendid tea, large bowls of soapy water and a plentiful supply of clay pipes, and left their guests to enjoy themselves. What joy to make bubble puddings by putting one's pipe into a bowl and just blowing without taking it out again, so long as one remembered not to suck! The triumph of gently shaking a particularly glorious bubble free of its pipe without bursting it, and watching it waft away, on a little summer breeze. The sheer magic prettiness of a flight of iridescent bubbles, blue and rose and gold, drifting through the tops of old quiet trees!

Elizabeth, Napier and Henry Crookenden belonged to the twelve-to-fourteen world. They kindly kept things going, but were not of the party. But Spencer, the youngest, was only nine, and also slightly short on friends of his own age, and just occasionally he noticed my existence, rather as a man throws a friendly word to a puppy in passing. Once he even gave me a cast-off but once precious book. I wish I had it still, but it got lost in one of our many moves. It was about a bachelor elf who lodged with a family of field mice. He was very untidy, and they almost asked him to leave; and then when the Terrible Day came, and the cornfield was invaded by harvesters, he rescued the mouse-children and got them to safety with such selfless gallantry that in gratitude, father and mother mouse asked him to make his home with them for ever more. There were pictures on every page, and the cover showed swaying ears of corn and huge scarlet poppies with petals of crumpled scarlet silk, and in the midst of them the doomed nest of woven grasses, and the bachelor elf sliding down a cornstalk with a mouse baby under one arm. I was grateful for Spencer's notice, but actually my two best friends of the Sheerness years were Spencer's father, and Gilson, my father's coxs'n.

Colonel Crookenden, was, I suppose, forty years older than me, a short, strongly-built man with a great hawk nose. His whole face, I later realised, would have looked very much at home under the embossed and crested helmet of a Roman general. The first time we ever met, after passing the time of day with my mother, he said to me, 'Come on, let's go,' and took my pushchair out of her hands and ran with me the full length of Sheerness High Street, my mother in hot pursuit. His hobby was making lead soldiers, and I soon had a sizeable private army, complete with despatch riders on motor-cycles and a stretcher party, to range alongside my toy farm on its green baize-covered board.

He called me Treacle, because in those days I was always called Honey, a joke which we both thought splendidly funny; and in later years I was invited to call him Crooky, a privilege he allowed to very few — and well do I remember his annoyance when one of his daughters-in-law called him Crooky without waiting to be invited!

I remember my mother, one hot summer's afternoon, holding forth to him on the subject of a company of soldiers she had just passed on their way in from route march, purple-faced in their tight upstanding collars. 'In this weather,' said my mother, 'why not collars undone, regulations or no regulations?'

'Look at my men, if you meet them coming in from route march,' said Crooky.

'Collars undone?'

'Collars undone and be damned to regulations.'

'You'll never make General,' said my mother.

'I know I won't,' said Crooky. And he never did.

Gilson, beside being coxs'n of my father's boat, did much the same kind of things about the house as an officer's batman often does in the Army. He looked after the boiler, groomed Don, cleaned shoes and silver, and always had time to play with me. I only had to shout down the basement stairs, and Gilson in a boiler-suit would come bounding up in the guise of a warhorse or a lion, or ready to be a whole ward full of wounded soldiers to my Florence Nightingale. Yet the water was always hot, and the shoes and silver and Don's black coat always shining. He must have been one of those very special people, beloved of the gods, for whom time is elastic and can always be stretched out to play with a child.

At the time, I think, I loved Gilson even more than Crooky. I certainly would not have thought of proposing to Crooky, even if there had not been a Mrs Crookenden, but when the time for leaving Sheerness drew near, I proposed to Gilson. He squatted on his heels in front of me and said not to make him laugh because he had a split lip. But though I looked very carefully, I could not see any split. Sadly, after we left Sheerness, he might have ceased to exist for all that I ever heard of him again. But when, only a few years ago, somebody asked me if I were suddenly to find myself the victim of *This is Your Life*, what long-lost friend out of my childhood I would like to see again, Gilson was the first person I thought of.

But oh, the bliss and splendour (Oh, poop poop! Oh my, oh my!) of just once being really noticed by the twelve-to-fourteens! It happened during the second of our Sheerness summers, when my cousins Edward and Enid came to stay. Edward was a Dartmouth cadet, tall, dark, lean, fascinatingly wicked, Enid a vivid, bird-boned creature who has lived on her nerves most of her life, but had not then begun to do so. Of course they hunted with their own age group, went on the car picnics and the jaunts up-river with Gilson; but when at home they noticed me! Especially Edward. The fair came to Sheerness while they were with us, and they all went to it, and Edward won a coconut and brought it back in triumph. My mother forbade me to have any, saying that it would be too indigestible. But Edward smuggled me a generous piece. I ate it to the last crumb, the only time that I have ever enjoyed coconut, and I was not sick.

Edward also spent quite a lot of time trying to teach me the Dartmouth version of *Fight the Good Fight*, wheeling me round and round the green in front of the terrace and joggling me violently up and down every time I lost the tune.

> Fight the good fight with all thy might,
> Sit on a barrel of dynamite,
> Light a match, and thou shalt see
> The quickest way to Eternit*ee*.

In my teens I suddenly developed quite a pretty singing voice and a reasonable ear, but at six I was as near to being tone deaf as makes no matter, so the jogglings were frequent, but much enjoyed by me. I was like a pup lying on its back and squirming for a human to rub its tummy, and Edward, in lordly fashion, always rubbed.

There was a rookery at the bottom of our garden, and through both the springs that we were there my mother collected the squabs that fell out of the nests and brought them up in hen-coops round the lawn. They were demons, and as soon as, wings clipped to keep them from flying away before they could fend for themselves, they were freed from the hen-coops, they all combined to make Don's life as much of a misery as possible. They stole his bones, and turned his water-bowl upside down and danced on it; and then had the gall to demand to share his warm and commodious kennel in the garden shed at night. Don put up with it all — he really was a saintly dog — and generally, when the back door was opened first thing in the morning, Don and the rooks, sitting bunched up against each other on the doorstep, would fall in a heap.

From those rooks' nests high in the treetops, there must have been a wonderful view over the dockyard and the town, and along the great curved sea walls, out over the marshes. Below the Adam houses and the walled gardens was the working part of the dockyard, whose smell of pitch and hot metal, wood and white paint, salt water and rope and oily smoke has remained for me the proper smell of ships and seafaring ever since, though most of such smells have disappeared long since. Outside the dockyard walls, through the gates with the bed of purple irises and the Metropolitan Police on guard, was the town and the barracks. But dockyard and town alike were very small; and beyond them, easily reached in a few minutes on foot, were the marshes.

When Ivy or my mother took me for a walk, we generally went one way or the other along the sea wall. If you turned to the left, after getting on to the wall, you followed a broad stone-built way between open estuary on one hand and a moat with swans trailing grey pennants of cygnets on the other. If you turned to the right you went along what I suppose was really 'Sheerness Front', until the wall sank and dwindled into a low sea defence among sand-dunes and marram grass, running on and on into the marsh. Don loved this way, because there were often courting couples to be found among the sand-dunes, and one of his favourite forms of sport was to creep up and bounce on them. At which times, my mother pretended he wasn't ours. I liked that way too, until the day she described to me how if we wandered from the causeway on to the sand, it might turn out to be quicksand; and I should be all right because the pushchair would keep me afloat (I do not, now, quite see why) but she would sink slowly, before my eyes, slowly, slowly, until the sand closed over — her — head. She was a magnificent actress. After that I was never quite happy on that stretch of the walls again.

But the rest of the marsh I loved. Especially I loved going out to tea with the Evans family, a retired captain and his wife and three grown-up daughters, who lived in a keeper's cottage right in the empty bird-haunted sky-reflecting wilds of it. Once, when we went there, they had been clearing out old boxes, and Mrs Evans had found her wedding-veil, and put it on to amuse me, and had tea in it. The lace and yellow-and-white wax orange-blossom must have looked a little strange on top of Mrs Evans's plump weather-beaten face, the grey hair she wore knotted up in an unfashionable bun, and the very workaday dress — Captain Evans, I think, had lost most of his pension in some way — but I thought she looked absolutely beautiful. Maybe I was right.

A retired Commander living in the town used occasionally

to take my mother and me for marsh runs in his car; and once, I think, he even took us on a Mr Openshaw trip when my father could not get away. From him, on a misty day out on the marshes, I heard a story of a great cloudy figure having lately been seen, over towards Minster, prowling and pawing and hovering, round the doors of two shepherds' cottages ...

That was all. No build-up, no follow-up — I was not frightened, but in my small bed in the house in Dockyard Terrace that night, I was glad I did not live out on the marsh, over towards Minster. Years later I gathered that Commander Bishop drank a good deal more than was good for him, but I don't think that was the explanation. I believe in his shadowy figures, if nobody else did. Even now, any sudden mist coming down brings the story and its own particular atmosphere back into my mind. The great fumbling figures, terrible and yet in some way pathetic, out of the mist and made of denser mist, pawing round the thresholds of living people.

In much that way, I felt later, when my mother first read *Beowulf* to me, Grendel must have come up from his marsh mists, pawing and snuffling round the doors of Heorot, hating the firelight and the harpsong that he longed to share; and the smell of Man. And when I came to write my own retelling of *Beowulf*, Commander Bishop's story had a little part to play in it.

In the autumn before my seventh birthday, the time came for leaving Sheerness; for parting with Don, who went to live with an old friend of my father's who had retired early and was fruit farming in another part of Kent; for parting with Crooky and Gilson who I still loved even though he would not marry me. Time for my father to go South Africa to join the cruiser *Birmingham* at Simonstown, while my mother and I went to spend the next eighteen months in rooms in Margate.

5

At this point, I feel that for my own sake, as much as for the sake of anyone reading this, I must deal with the aunts and uncles, to avoid confusion later.

We have never been a really united family. We do not have reunions, or flock round each other in times of crisis. We very seldom remember, or even know, each other's birthdays. But in my early years, aunts and uncles played a large part in my life, if only because they mostly lived fairly close at hand, and we went to visit them or had them to visit us, for the day, or the weekend, or on a leave that was too short for going back to my father's beloved Devon.

But first, of course, grandparents.

Grandmother Sutcliff was the only one I have ever known, all the rest having departed this life long before I was born. Having no grandfathers made me feel rather deprived. It seemed to me then, and has seemed to me ever since, that for a girl especially a grandfather is such a nice thing to have. And my one grandmother was so very disagreeable. If only I could have had the other grandmother instead, the one who hated menageries, and was a theosophist and believed in reincarnation, and once went to a dance in a cream-coloured gown with an enormous golden daffodil embroidered all up the front of the skirt. Grannie Sutcliff wore black, and I should think always had. Not smart black, but dusty black.

A gallant old thing, yes; she was nearing eighty by the time I knew her, my father being the last of a long and widely-spaced family. A tubercular hip in her teens, which remained rigid ever after, had not prevented her marrying a doctor and producing six babies; but undeniably she was as disagreeable as they come.

At the time I knew her she lived in a little house in a small select building estate called Onslow Village, just outside Guildford, with Mrs Harding who was short and fat for her cook, and Annie who was tall and gaunt for her housemaid. From Sheerness, and later from Chatham, we used to go and spend duty weekends with her now and then; when, there being only one spare room, I used to sleep on a camp bed in the corner, shut off from my parents by a screen which had long-legged cranes and sprays of pink pussy-willow on one side, and an all-over pattern that looked like going under chloroform on the other. Occasionally she called me her 'Chicky-Wee', which I loathed, but for the most part she called me a Noosence. She said all her grandchildren were Noosences, even the ones who by that time were rising thirty. She also said, constantly, even to my father's somewhat ruefully amused face, that she was a poor lone widow-woman and all her sons were dead.

Two of them were, as I have said before. Harvey, whose widow was Scottish Aunt Janet, had died of TB in the '14–'18 war, and Archie had died in the typhus camp at Wittenburg in the same war, having volunteered along with five other army doctors to go out to look after the British sick who had been simply left to die by the Germans. He and his wife, Natalie, a South African girl who I had little contact with at that time, were the producers of Edward and Enid. Grannie hated Janet and Natalie and Elizabeth my mother, because they had dared to marry her sons, even the one, my father, whom she hadn't wanted, didn't like, and had left to be brought up by his sisters, Aunt Maud, Aunt Edith and Aunt Lucy.

Aunt Edith was a handsome woman with straight thick brows which remained raven black even when her hair had turned swan's-wing white, and the bitterest mouth that I have ever seen on anybody. She, alas for them both, had married another Archie, weak-willed and amiable, who did not tell her beforehand that he was a quarter Indian — his mother being the product of an Indian Army colonel and a rajah's daughter — what would have happened if he had told Aunt Edith before it was too late, there's no knowing. Maybe she would still have married him, but I very much doubt it. As it was, finding out afterwards, she refused to have children — I very much doubt if she even allowed him into her bed! — and set out to make his life a cold hell to his dying day. I have been there at some family gathering myself, puzzled as a dog may be by stresses in the air, the electric discharge of things I did not understand, when he came into the room, and Aunt Edith sniffed loudly and said, 'There's a most peculiar smell in this room. One would almost think that somebody black had come into it.'

For many years, the family were quite seriously prepared for Uncle Archie to murder her one day, and prepared, if he did, to go into the witness-box on his behalf and swear that he did it under unendurable provocation.

Most surprisingly, in her last years, she mellowed, and for the first time she and my mother got on quite well. But that, of course, was too late for poor Uncle Archie.

Aunt Lucy was the widow of Aunt Janet's brother, who also died during the '14-'18 war. She was wizened like a long-biding apple, and wore a wig, which I regarded with a hideous fascination, and was the mother of one wretched henpecked son who departed to the Malay States at the earliest possible moment. She had been a VAD in the war, and with my passionate interest in all things medical — I think but for the Still's Disease I would have added another doctor, the first female of the species, to the family — I loved the stories that she had to tell, even though I never loved her very much. My father said staunchly that she had been pretty as a girl and I never believed him, until, years after she was dead, we were going through a mass of old photographs, and found one of the assembled cast of a pantomime presented by the Torrington Amateur Dramatic Society years before, and there in the group was Aunt Lucy, unmistakably Aunt Lucy, and really quite pretty!

I owe Aunt Lucy something, for if Sheerness gave me my love of marsh country, it was because of her that I first came to know and love the South Downs.

Aunt Lucy lived in one of the new housing estates that had just begun to sprawl up over the downs from the old coastwise villages east of Brighton. Hers was the first house in her road, small and jerry-built and villa-ish. In front of it was the unmade chalk road, and piles of wood and brick and rubble, and the embryos of several more small, jerry-built, villa-ish houses; but behind, immediately outside the gate of the raw little garden, were the downs. The downs much as they must have been in the days when Kipling was living at Rottingdean, only a couple of miles away. Much as they must have been, come to that, at the time when he wrote of them in his heartbreaking story 'The Knife and the Naked Chalk'.

My first memory of them, dating, I suppose, from the first of our Sheerness summers, is of sitting on the ground outside that gate. I was in disgrace. Aunt Lucy was frugal, to put it mildly; visits to her were only survived by the making of secret forays into Saltdean to buy buns; and she was not a very good cook. At this particular lunchtime I had refused to eat my pudding, on the grounds that it both looked and tasted pale grey. I had not meant to be rude; the pudding did look and taste pale grey, and I was simply giving her the true and valid reason for my refusal to eat it. But social lessons had to be learned; one cannot go through life telling one's hostess that her pudding is pale grey, even when it is. So there I sat in disgrace outside her back gate. It was quite safe to leave me there because, though by that time I could walk a little, my knees were set rigid and I could not get up without help, so I was securely tethered from wandering off and coming to any sort of harm. And there I was to wait, until somebody came and opened the gate and asked me if I was sorry, and took me back into civilised society.

But I did not feel in disgrace, and I was in no hurry to be forgiven and taken back. I was perfectly happy where I was, I was discovering downland turf for the first time. As we grow older, we forget how near to the ground we once were. I do not mean merely because our heads were lower down than they are now, though of course that comes into it; but near in the sense of kinship. A small child is aware of the sights and smells and textures of the ground with an acute awareness that we lose in growing up. So I sat outside Aunt Lucy's gate, with my legs stuck straight out in front of me, and investigated and experienced to my heart's content the foot or two of world going on around me. Pink and white convolvulus smelling of almond paste rambled along the foot of my aunt's raw new fence; and the turf itself was not just grass, but a densely interwoven forest of thyme and scarlet pimpernel, creamy honey-scented clover and cinquefoil and the infinitely small and perfect eye-bright with the spot of celestial yellow at its heart; all held close to the ground on stems less than an inch high, which is the result of a few hundred years of cropping by downland sheep.

And I, looking down into the forest, and yet at the same time feeling its tall matted overgrowth meeting above my head, watched a tiny metallic green beetle climbing industriously up one grass blade and down another, found a yellow-banded snail-shell, caught a seven-spot ladybird that lingered on my hand for a moment before flying away. Later, for I must in fact be remembering a blend of many afternoons after that first one spent sitting outside

Aunt Lucy's gate without having first been rude about her pudding, I learned to put heads of rye-grass up one sleeve of my cotton frock, for the sake of enduring the delicious tickling agony as they crept across my shoulders and down the other sleeve. Later, also, somebody, I have no idea who, showed me how to make dolls in red petticoats by turning back the crinkled scarlet silk petals of the little field poppies and tying them in at the waist with a blade of grass, then sticking a thicker stem through just below the seed head for their outstretched arms.

Above all, I soaked in the 'feel' of the downs, the warm sense of the ground itself actively holding one up; a sureness, a steadfastness; and the sense that one gets in down country of kinship with a land that has been mixed up with the life of men since it and men began.

Thank you, Aunt Lucy, for your pale grey pudding.

Aunt Maud, my father's eldest sister, was fat. Not fat like a full-blown rose, but fat like a feather-bed. She had married yet another doctor — Uncle Ted; who looked, apart from the fact that he was very tall, exactly like Charles I, and, despite that king's reputation for virtue so said family tradition, with good reason. (I suppose it could have been a father's likeness inherited through Charles II.) He was the one and only doctor in Ripley — the one near Guildford, not the one in Yorkshire — where they lived in a house now primly called The Lindens, which, behind its polite Georgian façade, had once been a pub. Aunt Maud, like some kind of cosy magnet, kept the family together to the day of her death, after which it fell apart and never came together again. At The Lindens one met far-flung cousins one never met anywhere else. It was, I think, in my early days the only place where we ever met Aunt Edith.

In the room where I slept at The Lindens the sole ornament on the mantelpiece was a papier-mâché cow, whose head, appearing out of a round hole in its shoulders, nid-nodded every time a lorry rumbled by on the Portsmouth road. I think I was only in the drawing-room twice, for a couple of family weddings; I do not think it was used at any other time, except for sleeping in on Christmas afternoons. There was a long dining-room with heavy oak furniture and a portrait of King Charles, believed to be by Lely; and a surgery which got rather gory and dramatic on Saturday nights, because in those days no one called an ambulance to a car smash, they merely hauled the victims off to the nearest doctor. Except for mealtimes, life went on in the big old-fashioned kitchen, around Aunt Maud and Lois the cook, who had been with the family since she was twelve.

My mental picture of that kitchen shows it crowded, and the crowd includes the two sons of the house, Phil (dark) and Ted (fair) wandering in and out, Ettie (thin and acid) and Connie (plump and laughing), the two elder daughters, and Joy, the baby of the family by a long way, still at school and having a crush on the games mistress, about which everyone teased her unmercifully, doing mountains of prep at one end of the kitchen table. Probably Aunt Edith would be knitting in the window; she was always knitting. Some people said that her spiritual home was the foot of the guillotine. Occasionally Uncle Ted would be there, though truth to tell, the only two things I really remember of Uncle Ted are his likeness to the portrait in the dining-room (which for years I thought was him in fancy dress) and the fact that, much taken with my fondness for long words, he taught me to say Encephalitis Lethargica.

There is a gramophone somewhere in the picture, too, the property of the younger generation, with a horn like an enormous convolvulus flower; though I think that it was most often borne off to the privacy of a bedroom, and me with it for a treat, to churn out tinny renderings of Jessie

Matthews singing 'Spread a Little Happiness' and excerpts from *The Mikado*.

And in the midst of everything, no matter what went on around her, sat Aunt Maud, panting lightly and eating everything, especially chocolate, which came her way. I suppose it isn't really any wonder that she died when I was only nine.

Ripley was something of a Sutcliff stronghold. Next door to The Lindens lived Aunt Esther and Aunt Carry, of an older generation, in a house with potted palms and a canary in the drawing-room. It was a house which had, and needed, no name of its own; and which, when it was sold after their deaths, went on the market simply as "The Misses Sutcliffs' House'. Further down the village, The Clock House, even then become an hotel, was once the house of my father's Uncle Joe, who was the Ripley doctor before Uncle Ted. He came there as a young assistant to a still earlier doctor, and Lord Onslow being taken ill while the real doctor was away, Uncle Joe coped with the situation, and won such golden opinions that the Onslows took him up and determined to find a wife for him. They got down all the unmarried girls of their acquaintance whom they considered suitable, one after another, as it were on appro, until, so says tradition, one of them rang the bell. Uncle Joe called on her with a bouquet of pelargoniums, and she became Aunt Katie, the Aunt Katie, long since widowed, whom I mentioned before as coming to see me with either biscuits or doll's furniture when I was ill.

My mother's contribution to the family consisted of three elder brothers, Uncle Harold, Uncle Cyril and Uncle Acton, the Bad Penny.

Uncle Harold, when not in India, that is to say, when on leave and after he retired, lived in Dorset with his wife Aunt Kythé. At least, they shared the same roof, and had actually produced a son, Graeme, but that was a long time ago. When I knew him, Graeme was already at Oxford, a tall, wilting young man with a lock of tow-coloured hair always falling over one eye. His elders said he was a young puppy. Later, he became a darling. But even then, on the few occasions I met him, he was always a darling to me.

There was a strong bond of affection between Uncle Harold and my mother, the eldest and the youngest of the family. They had a great deal in common, including the instinct for the dramatic which has always cropped up from time to time in the Lawton line. They both saw themselves as Tragic Figures, he because of Aunt Kythé, my mother because of me. And they both, at least part of the time, enjoyed the sight. My uncle's marriage was not a happy one, but as Aunt Kythé spent virtually her whole waking life at her bridge club, and so even when he was at home their paths seldom crossed, I cannot but feel that the instinct for drama was at work when he once remarked that the only thing that made life worth living was the knowledge that there was death at the end of it. He was the only person, except my mother, whom I have actually seen sitting at the breakfast table, with his head in his hands, eyes closed in a mask of tragedy, for no other reason — at least, none discernible to anybody else — than that the telephone bill had come in or the slugs had been at the lupins.

I wish he could have had my mother's gift for laughter, at the other end of the scale. For when she was happy, she was as happy as a lark; and if he had had more laughter in him he might have had more times of happiness, too. But I suppose he did, in his much more sober way. He had a quiet and unpredictable humour of his own; and there were things that he enjoyed doing. Especially he loved scouring Dorset and the New Forest, visiting and revisiting old haunts; and when we were staying with him, we scoured far and wide, in his car while he was still driving, in ours after he had given it up. Purbeck and the Tarrant Valley, Cranborne Chase and the Cerne Giant and Buckler's Hard all knew us, and we came back to them again and again, lovingly, in his company. Then, too, he collected pewter, and old broken-down clocks and watches in the hopes of one day putting them together again, though he never did; and books from the 6d trays outside bookshops: books on India, as one would expect, but also battered little volumes of fairy-tales, and anything he could find that had to do with gypsies. He was a mine of information on the Romany tongue, which he maintained had certain strong points of likeness with Sanskrit. He taught me my passion for Kipling even, I think, before my mother did — he was incredibly like Kipling in appearance, except for the spectacles — and in his lesser way he too was a story-teller. When I was in bed at night, in the tiny back bedroom that Aunt Kythé called the Rose Room because of the rose-patterned chintz curtain masking off the half of it which was in fact the boxroom, he would come up and sit on the side of the bed, and in his quiet, rather pedantic voice, weave stories of the places where we had been that day, and the evil doings of himself and his brothers when they were young; and above all stories of India, of how he had once seen a real 'mongoose-kill-cobra' fight, not in the bazaar for pice, but in the jungle for free; of railway building, his native workmen and Eurasian overseers, and the day a train came by carrying mysterious cases suspected of containing guns, but which, on investigation, turned out to be full of superb brass dragons stamped 'Made in Birmingham'; wonderful stories too, of an older India than his, of Mogul Emperors and the Mutiny.

My Uncle Cyril was not unlike Don Quixote in build, long and lean and stooping, with a nose which had caused him in his young days to be called 'Beaky Iddle' by his brothers and sisters. He had left India only halfway through his career, to join a firm of consulting engineers; and he and Aunt Gladys and their two sons when they were at home lived in the last house in a suburban road with nothing but fields beyond them all the way to Wallingham. At least, that was how it was when I first remember them. For many years now it has been sunk without trace in a wilderness of trim roads lined with blotting-paper-pink flowering cherries, and each house and each road exactly like the next; so that I could never imagine how Uncle Cyril found his way home from the office in the evenings. As long as a rose could be scraped up anywhere in the garden from the first buds of May to the frost-browned lastlings of November, he set out every morning with a rose in his buttonhole in a little silver holder; and he tipped like a prince — half-a-crown at a time, which I found almost an embarrassment because it was so much that I did not really know what to do with it, and all too often ended by putting it in my money-box, which seemed a poor-spirited sort of thing to do with a tip. He had no stories of India, seeming to have left that part of his life all behind him when he came home. He seemed to have left an awful lot of himself behind him, somewhere along the way, though he loved Aunt Gladys and was a much happier person than Uncle Harold; which is maybe why I really remember so little about him.

Which brings me to the Bad Penny, about whom I remember a great deal.

Uncle Acton spent the whole of his working life in India for the simple reason that he gave up work very young. He was always on the point of going back to India, his family used to pray that he would go back. Several times he had his passage booked; but somehow he never went.

Building Indian roads was not really the life for my Uncle Acton. He would have done superbly well in one of those pierrot troupes with black pom-poms down the front of their loose white smocks that one used to see and hear on any beach worth the name — so long as the rest of the troupe could have kept him sober for performances and barred him from being the one to carry round the hat afterwards. My father, who had a sneaking affection for him, as many people had, maintained that there was one thing to be said for Acton: he never cadged. My mother, whose bicycle he had taken and sold when she was at school, said he had no need to cadge, he merely helped himself. He could, quite seriously, have made his living with perfect ease on the halls, for he was fat and funny and could conjure music out of anything from a wash-board to a length of hosepipe. He played the banjo (Kipling's 'War drum of the White Man, round the World') and, really beautifully, the Hawaiian guitar. One does not hear either very often nowadays, but I never hear them, especially the Hawaiian guitar, without remembering Uncle Acton playing, generally 'Waikiki, War Chant' or a very fancy rendering of 'Bye bye, Blackbird'. Without remembering also the little bungalow lost in the pinewoods above Headley Down, where my mother and I spent six weeks at his invitation, after my father went to South Africa.

6

On the way to Headley Down, as it were, I spent a couple of weeks in a nursing-home in London, while Mr Openshaw did manipulations under anaesthetic to my knees.

The days of being given a prick in the arm in an ante-room and told to count, before being wheeled along to the theatre in a warm stupor on a rubber-tyred trolley, had not yet arrived. One walked in stone-cold sober on one's own flat feet, and lay down on the operating table and had a mask put over one's face.

Given a kinder one than ether, I still think that an inhaled anaesthetic such as gas and oxygen, and the human contact of the anaesthetist's hand against one's face, and his voice saying quietly, 'Breathe deeply. Deeply. That's right, that's splendid …' is a better way of going under than a jab in the arm and a lonely shoot-off into spinach-green oblivion.

But I digress.

I walked in my blue dressing-gown into a bright white room full of curious objects, and was greeted with kindly courtesy by Mr Openshaw and my anaesthetist, both of them white-robed, but neither as yet masked. I had been very curious as to who would give me my anaesthetic; and my mother, I suppose to give me the reassuring feeling that what was going to happen was nothing very important, had told me that she expected it would be a medical student.

'How shall I know if it's a medical student?' I asked.

'Ask him,' said my mother.

So when I was met by a tall and distinguished-looking man with grey hair, who, had I but known it, was one of the foremost anaesthetists of his day, I shook hands warmly, and looked up with interest into his face. 'Please, sir,' said I (in the service world in which I had been brought up, all the boys called the grown men 'sir', and the girls caught it from them), 'please, sir, are you a medical student?'

'I was once,' he said, 'and I suppose I always shall be.'

He picked me up and put me on the table, and the last thing I felt as the waves of ether washed over me was the warm quiet reassuring pressure of his hand against the side of my face.

When I left the nursing-home Uncle Acton met us at Victoria Station so that we should travel down together. He was extremely drunk. At the time, I just thought he seemed a little odd, blurred in both his speech and his legs, but when I showed friendly concern he said it was just a touch of his old malaria and would soon pass. I could not think why my mother looked so white and worried.

Anyhow, we arrived safely, to be met with gentle kindness by Miss Edes.

Miss Edes and Uncle Acton had an 'Understanding'. They had had it for twenty years, during which Miss Edes had loved Uncle Acton truly and faithfully, and he, I think, had found it pleasant and convenient to be so loved. The Understanding never blossomed into an engagement; my uncle was not the marrying kind, but he contrived during those years to spoil all Miss Edes's chances of marrying anybody else. And there must, I am sure, have been chances, for she was charming in a quiet way, intelligent, musical, kind, capable, loving. Much too good for Uncle Acton in fact. My mother tried to make her see that he simply wasn't worth it. But, alas, we do not love people for their worthiness to be loved. It's possible, of course, that the world would be a colder place if we did.

It was with Miss Edes and her fat dragon of a mother that we were going to lodge in Margate, or rather in Westgate nearby while my father was in South Africa. But meanwhile, Uncle Acton had had this rather happy idea of renting the little bungalow called La Delicia for six weeks, and installing Miss Edes and my mother and me. An 'Understanding' did not at that time mean living together, and though he would be in London all the week, he would be coming down at weekends, so it would be useful to have my mother there as chaperone. Apart from attacks of malaria, which recurred with regrettable frequency, it all worked out very happily indeed; and those weeks have always stuck in my memory as a time folded in on itself, a little bit of life quite separate from the rest and faintly magical.

We arrived a few days before the 5th of November, and Uncle Acton decided that we should have our own fireworks party, since I had never experienced one before, and went into Hazlemere to buy the fireworks. The night came, clear and with a touch of frost to mingle with the scent of pine trees and wood smoke in the air; exactly what a Guy Fawkes' night ought to be. And my mother and Miss Edes and I wrapped in rugs were installed in the open-sided garden shed, while Uncle Acton took his stand with his box of fireworks on the patch of rough lawn in front of us. I had confided to him the fact that I did not like bangs (even crackers at Christmas parties were a source of dread to me at that time, as I think they are to more children than ever admit to it), and he had promised that there should be absolutely no bangs. Being innocent, I trusted him, and gazed upon the box of fireworks with nothing but the anticipation of delight. I should have known better. The first firework went off with an earsplitting series of bangs, and I took off nearly through the roof of the garden shed. When he had done with mock apologies and crazy explanations as to how the banger had got in with the rest, he got on with his display: silver fountains, golden rain, whirling and whizzing Catherine-wheels, flowers of flame and eruptions of coloured stars, all accompanied by the prancings and patter, the clowning and the showmanship that were so much a part of my uncle. And after that first one, not another bang. But for me, I can't say it was all spoiled by that first bang, nothing could really spoil the magic of fireworks dancing and sparkling and coruscating against the darkness of pine trees in a frosty dusk, but I certainly held on very tight to my seat through the whole performance, waiting for the next.

That was the only real happening which I connect with our weeks on Headley Down. The rest is more a kind of blanket memory, of place and atmosphere and tiny events often repeated. La Delicia sat in a kind of little bay of the pine woods; with open common, furze and bracken and the dead brown wreck of last summer's heather in front, and the trees crowding close to the windows on its other three sides — twisted fir trees like old men with long crooked fingers in an Arthur Rackham illustration. My memory says that the woods around were all pine trees, but there must be a mistake somewhere, because I also have a picture of finding acorns among fallen leaves and dark friable leaf-mould. Big fat acorns turning chestnut brown, and already splitting to send out tiny crimson shoots.

Squirrels chittered at us from behind branches, red squirrels lilting from branch to branch in the autumn sunlight like wisps of wind-torn flame. It seemed to be always sunny; hoar frost every morning and red sunsets every night. There was one special road my mother and I used to take often in the afternoons, to watch the sun go down like a great rose-red balloon behind the trees of the next ridge; then hurry home, keeping well to the middle of the road, out of reach of the tree-men who were particularly Rackhamish in that part of the woods, to tea and hot buttered toast with Miss Edes, and Uncle Acton's Hawaiian guitar if it was the weekend.

Not only weekends, come to think of it, because as time passed, he went up to London less and less often. He had developed a peculiar toe (gout?) and one day when he did go up about his business, whatever that might be, he went in one brown shoe with a trap-door cut in it to accommodate a bunion, and one plaid carpet-slipper worn over a yellow bedsock.

There was the day my mother took me into Headley, shopping, and parked me as usual in my pushchair outside the grocer's while she went in. The window of this particular shop had been sprinkled with dead flies since the time of our first visit and presumably since the summer, but there must have been a pre-Christmas clear-out, and they were gone. I was deeply interested in this circumstance, and felt that it deserved notice — everybody's notice. So I called the news to my mother inside. 'Oh, Mummy! Mummy! Do look! They've taken all the dead flies out of the window.'

I was not popular.

I was not popular, either, the day Uncle Acton came down from London driving a new sports car. Well, new to him, anyway. He always drove brightly-coloured sports cars. I think maybe he had Walter Mitty dreams of being another Malcolm Campbell, and always gave them fancy names. One had actually been called Bluebird. This one, he told me, was called Yellowhammer. It was, like all his cars, extremely dirty, for his love did not extend to cleaning them; and I had just been listening to my mother's private comments on the subject. 'Mummy says,' I told him, 'that you had much better call it the Mudlark.'

I meant no harm, I thought it was funny and merely wished to share the joke. But Uncle Acton was deeply wounded, and my mother was furious. 'You are a horrid little girl,' she said, 'and I will never tell you anything, ever again.'

As my memories of Malta are strung together by the sound of bells, so my memories of Headley Down are strung together on smells. The smell of leaf-mould and pine woods and bonfire smoke and frost; and above all, of lamp smitch. La Delicia was lit by oil lamps, whose care and cleaning was left to my mother and Miss Edes, neither of whom understood much more about lamps than I do about aerial navigation. So the lamps always smoked; and even now, the smell of lamp smitch, which most people find unpleasant, is to me one of those magic smells which open doorways in the mind, letting out the sights and sounds and other smells of some place and time which might otherwise, little by little, be lost and forgotten.

7

We left La Delicia, and the pine woods with the twisted old men's fingers and the scent of frost and wood smoke, on my seventh birthday, and went to lodge with Miss Edes and her unspeakable mama on the cold north Kentish coast. One bedroom and a living-room, use of bathroom, complete with geyser whose volcanic noises full of menace worked on my fear of bangs and made bath nights a time of dread lest it was going to blow up.

And for outdoors, until we got to know our way around, there was only the front, mainly populated by spinal carriages and their pushers. Nobody sound in wind and limb was fool enough to be out in those winds, straight, as the natives proudly informed us, from the North Pole. A spinal carriage was a kind of wicker coffin on wheels, with a pram handle at one end, in which one lay flat, or very uncomfortably sat up, during sitting-up sessions. They were the most uncomfortable and the coldest form of transport ever invented. I know, I had one.

When the winds along the front were too much even for us, which is saying something for my mother was a fresh-air fiend, we went inland along the roads and ways and avenues of the harsh little seaside town. Oh, how I remember the grey, bitter afternoons leading up to that first Christmas! How we lingered to look in at lighted windows, warming ourselves at the ruddy glow of light through cosily drawn curtains, or if the curtains were not yet drawn, glimpsing sometimes a Christmas tree hung with baubles, or the flicker of a fire; much like Mole and Ratty wandering through the village in *The Wind in the Willows*. But we had neither Mole End nor River Bank to go home to; only our rather dreary and so far impersonal 'rooms'. I used to imagine, even hope a little, that somebody would look up and see us in the dusk beyond their windows, and fling open their front door and come with hands held out, crying, 'You poor darlings! Come in! Come in to the fire and share our Christmas tree!' I think in a way my poor mother must have shared that dream. But we had as yet no friends in Westgate. No door flew open, and we trundled back to our own tea in our rooms. Probably perfectly warm and adequately hot-buttered-toasted, but lonely because we missed my father. I still think it would have been nice if one of those doors had been flung open ...

The time of desolation did not last so very long. Before spring we had made friends. One friend each, anyway. Giles Dixon and his mother.

Mrs Dixon had honey-coloured hair. Giles had TB glands in his neck, and a spinal carriage like mine. Mr Dixon came down from London at weekends, but during the week they too were on their own, and we got into the way of going for our daily walks together. Giles was two years younger than me, and owned a grey flannel horse called Galloping Gus, which he would share with me sometimes. That, come to think of it, was generous of him, because I never shared Pip, my lop-eared black dog, with anybody.

Generally on the outward half of our walks we would both have to lie flat, our view made up of racing skies and roof-tops and streaming branches and circling gulls. But on the way home we were allowed to sit up and communicate; and sometimes, though not often, we had tea with each other. Hundreds-and-thousands on brown bread and butter, and the pleasure of each other's company.

With Giles and his mother, who had lived in Westgate a long time and knew all the best walks, we discovered the delights of the Dent du Leon Farm. The Dent du Leon had the special enchantment that comes of being hidden and unexpected. To reach it, you went along an ordinary little road between ordinary little houses with nothing to differentiate between it and any other of its kind, except the strong smell of gas. The road appeared to be a cul-de-sac, ending in a field fence. But if you braved the smell of gas and continued undaunted to the very end, suddenly between the last house and the fence there was a narrow track running off to the right in a conspiratorial sort of manner. Soon the fence stopped, and the track became a real country field-path, and ran on on its own, skirting a wide meadow. And at the end of the path, on the far side of the meadow, was the warm brown huddle of farm buildings.

There was no farmhouse; I suppose there must have been a house and more buildings somewhere else. But it possessed what few farm steadings possess, the remains of a Norman gatehouse — at least, I was told that it was a Norman gatehouse, and in view of the name it seems likely — with lancet windows full of sky, and valerian and wild wallflowers growing in the cracks of the crumbling masonry. Also it possessed a kind of sunken pit full of pigs, very dirty and pig-smelling pigs, but companionable, and always ready and willing to have their backs scratched with a stick. Giles loved the pigs. I loved them too, but only because Giles did, and so my love was really secondhand. But the Norman gatehouse I loved with a firsthand love that was all my own.

It must have been early spring the first time we came that way, because in my memory the verge of the field-path is always starred with shining galaxies of lesser celandines. As we took walks that way for eighteen months, spring, summer, autumn and winter, this cannot have been so in dull and sober fact. So most probably the celandines belong to the first time that ever I went that way, and the shining vision has remained.

Giles was a terrific character. Imprisoned in his spinal

carriage and only allowed out for one hour's exercise a day, it was incredible the things he managed to cram into that hour. The first few minutes would be almost painful to watch, even to me at seven, as he tore round the garden in a series of frog-hops, flailing his arms and shouting in his desperate need to get rid of the surplus energy of the past twenty-three bottled-up hours, somewhat like a kettle with its lid about to blow off. But that safely accomplished, he set about other things. Such as gardening. He had a little bright red wheelbarrow in which he trundled things methodically from place to place. Things of all kinds, including snails. Giles's fondness for snails started one day when he was very naughty; so naughty that the fairies turned his goldfish into snails in the night. But the fairies had underestimated the breadth of Giles's interests and his ability to receive new ones at the drop of a hat. Confronted with two snails sitting in the bottom of the goldfish bowl, and the news that the fairies would not be returning them to their proper shapes until he had been a good boy for a whole week, Giles was simply delighted. He had never appreciated snails at their proper worth before but, having them brought to his notice in this way, he became a snail addict thenceforward. He generally managed to have a few, gathered in that precious hour of freedom, secreted about himself. But on one particular occasion he had larger ideas. He collected a whole regiment of snails, piling them into his little red barrow and getting them into the house despite the vigilance of his mother and the maid, parked them under the stairs. It is surprising how far snails can travel in a single night, when nothing happens to upset them or break their concentration, and by morning they had reached to the uttermost ends of the house, leaving their silvery slime-trails behind them across carpets and cushions, walls and ceilings. And it was no good even calling on the fairies to magic Giles's goldfish back again, because he liked snails better than goldfish, anyway.

Once, Giles's mother had to go up to London for the day, leaving him at home with the maid. Giles was disgusted, and said he was planning to be a pink cloud and live in a bird's nest and have no more worries. I know exactly how he felt: very much as I do to this day, when I announce loudly to a world that has got too much for me that I am going to join the Foreign Legion.

During most of the time I knew him Giles had his head and neck heavily bandaged, which was then part of the treatment for TB glands; and his hair, on the few occasions I saw it, was the palest bleached sand colour. But towards the end of our time in Westgate it was decided that he was now well enough to have the bandages off. His hair leapt joyously to meet the light, like a flower brought out from a dark cellar; and within a few weeks it was a deep and fiery red, as though it too was bursting with its owner's pent-up energy.

My other close friend at Westgate was Mrs Wayne. She belongs mainly to the summer time and sea front. She was I suppose in her late seventies, an imposing figure topped by a shady black hat and sitting in an enormous wicker bath-chair. Her small meagre companion used to park the bath-chair on the front in the sunshine, and go off to do the morning's shopping. I do not remember how Mrs Wayne and I became bosom friends, but after it happened, my mother used to park me alongside her, and go off to do her shopping also.

Mrs Wayne was a woman of her hands, and therein lay her chief fascination, for I was already beginning to be a woman of mine. I cannot now remember one word that passed between us, though I imagine we chatted a good deal. But I remember the comfortable companionship, and

the things she made, sitting there in her bath-chair in some
sheltered corner of the front. Chiefly they were tea-cosies
and straw hats. The tea-cosies were always of the 'cottage'
variety, and I have never since seen a cottage tea-cosy to
equal them. They had thatched roofs of golden-brown raffia
couched down in the traditional patterns of the thatcher's
art. Their walls of rough cream linen were richly and
lovingly embroidered with green front doors, and windows
with green shutters, and a riot of flowers in the bed that
ran round the bottom. Climbing roses rambled up the walls,
and generally a cat sat on a doorstep or windowsill. They
were thickly padded, and gave a wonderful impression of
home and shelter. I would have loved to live in one of Mrs
Wayne's tea-cosies.

But it was in her hats that Mrs Wayne really let herself
go. She did not actually make them, she bought plain
rough straw hats and turned them into things of splendour
and enchantment. Scarlet poppies and cornflowers and
marguerites and nodding ears of corn made harvest festival
round them, not merely embroidered on, but in some
magical way free-standing. But the loveliest of all had crab-
apples on them, made by winding string round and round
a pencil until a little ball had been formed; then sliding it
carefully off the pencil and oversewing it with yellow and
red and green and russet raffia, up through the hole in the
centre, spread smoothly and carefully down over the ripe
outside curve, up through the centre again ... lastly a clove
stuck into one end of the hole, before the apple was added
to the spray on the stupendous hat. I used to get nearer
and nearer in eager interest, until my nose was virtually
hooked over her arm, and I must have been in grave danger
of getting pricked. I must also have been somewhat of an
inconvenience at times. But Mrs Wayne never complained.
Maybe she did not even want to complain; there is, after all,

something rather pleasant in the knowledge that a child is spellbound in one's company, especially, maybe, when one is rising eighty.

It seems to me now surprising that with so much else going on, I was also having lessons. Or more truthfully, sitting through lessons with practically nothing to show for them afterwards. That was not my mother's fault. She tried so hard; she had begun trying when we first went to Sheerness, and had been at it ever since. Actually, I had absorbed quite a lot. Under the heading of General Knowledge, I think I would have done quite well in a TV quiz. I knew the meaning of the three white bands round a sailor's collar, I knew the proportions of an iceberg above and below water, and the name of Apollo's mother. From a lovely book about a little boy going on a voyage round the world with his toys, which I had on long loan from grown-up cousins (very long loan; I have it still) I had accumulated quite a lot of geography. From *Flower Fairies of the Seasons* I had gathered nearly as much botany as I have now; and I seldom find myself at a loss where flowers and trees are concerned. I had a smattering of child's-version history from *Our Island Story*, in which Queen Boadicea rebelled against the Romans because they had beaten her and been rude to her daughters. But I could add two and two together three times and get a different answer each time. And I could not do the one thing on which everything else depended.

I could not read.

Neither could Rudyard Kipling until he was nine years old; but neither my mother nor I knew that at the time; and my mother was at times near to despair. My failure really was her fault, for the odd reason that she herself read too well and too willingly. I have noticed that a child who has a willing adult to read to him is often late in learning to read to himself, simply because, when being read to, he can cope with stories well in advance of those he could read for himself; and so learning to read means, in an odd sort of way, a step backwards. My mother started to read to me when I was very young indeed. She read aloud beautifully and never got tired, and she would never, from the first, read anything that she could not enjoy herself, which cut out all the poor quality writing which every right-minded child loves when he can get it. Her only concession was one weekly comic, *Rainbow*. But apart from that, I was reared on a fine mixed diet of Beatrix Potter, A A Milne, Dickens, Stevenson, Hans Andersen, Kenneth Grahame and Kipling — especially *Puck of Pook's Hill* whose three magnificent stories of Roman Britain were the beginning of my own passion for the subject, and resulted in the fullness of time in *The Eagle of the Ninth*. Hero myths of Greece and Rome I had, in an unexpurgated edition which my mother edited herself as she went along, and Norse and Saxon and Celtic legends. There were Whyte Melville's *The Gladiators* and Bulwer Lytton's *Last Days of Pompeii* and Weigal's *Egyptian Princess*; for my mother loved historical novels — history of any kind, though her view of it was always the minstrel's rather than the historian's.

When I was about six, she decided that the time had come for me to learn to read. And that was when she made her mistake. Instead of merely sitting me down in front of *Peter Rabbit*, *The Secret Garden* or the *Jungle Books* and telling me to get on with it, she provided a dreadful book about a Rosy-Faced Family who Lived Next Door and Had Cats that Sat on Mats, and expected me to get on with that. I was outraged — I, who had walked the boards with the Crummles, and fought beside Beowulf in the darkened Hall of Heriot. I took one look, and decided that the best way of making sure that I should never meet the Rosy-Faced Family or any of their unspeakable kind in the future was not to learn to read at all. So I didn't, and my mother never quite had the hardness of heart to stop reading to me. We had lessons and lessons and lessons; and we got practically nowhere.

She did take to reading me *The Little Matchgirl* rather more frequently as time went on. Maybe she hoped that I would learn to read as a means of avoiding that particular story, but I have a nasty suspicion that it was done as a means of providing light relief for herself, because *The Little Matchgirl* always made me cry.

I must explain.

My mother was the perfect Spartan mother. I have always been able to imagine her telling her sons to return from battle 'with their shields, or on them'. She did actually try it on my father at the start of the Second World War. He didn't take it kindly, and confided to me ruefully that he thought she rather fancied herself as a Hero's Widow. But she hadn't any sons, she only had me. So I was brought up under rigid naval discipline. My mother demanded instant unquestioning and unflinching obedience. I have heard her boast to friends that if she had told me to put my hand in the fire, I would have done it. I wonder if I would. When I was bad, I received corporal punishment; five hard smacks on my behind. I took my punishment in silence, and was a little proud of myself that I did so. The only thing I resented was the fact that she always told people she gave me three smacks; and it was five! I am not saying that corporal punishment and attendant pride in taking it in silence are good things, I am merely saying that that was how it was; just as I am not advocating such rigid discipline. I think my mother was too strict and my upbringing too hard; but I do not think it did me any real harm. Maybe some of it actually helped me in later years.

But included in this boy's upbringing was a boy's attitude

to tears. I was brought up to the idea that there was something shameful about crying — unless my mother was doing it, that was different. 'Boys don't cry' was so much a part of my training that by the time I was sixteen or seventeen, I couldn't cry. Or rather, crying had become as rare and difficult and painful for me as it is for most men of my own and my father's generations, and it has remained so ever since, denying me the relief and safety valve that like most people I have sometimes sorely needed. But at six or seven or eight I had not yet reached this stage. I could dissolve into tears as easily as anybody else of my age. But I had learned, learned to the marrow of my bones, that crying was shameful. Therefore I had developed a trick, when cry I must, of casting my eyes up to Heaven, and holding them wide open, in the rather piteous hope that this would somehow make room for the tears to run down inside my face, and nobody would know that I was crying. It was years before I learned that the idea was never going to work; and so all the family thought that the sight of Honey crying was hilariously funny, and my mother, with no idea of the truth, found it the funniest of all, and used to describe it as my 'Oh Lord! How long?' face, and continued to read me *The Little Matchgirl*.

My poor mother, she thought to her dying day that she knew and always had known everything there was to know about me.

We struggled on with the reading lessons. And then, how or why it came about, I do not know, Betty Evans, one of the daughters from the cottage on Sheerness Marshes, was living next door; and it seemed that she was a trained governess. So I began doing lessons with her. Dear Betty Evans, gentle and gay and sweet and patient. I enjoyed my mornings with her, but I don't think she had much more luck than my mother; and the chief thing I remember about those lessons is that she taught me how to make little woolly creatures, a big puff-ball of wool for the body, a smaller one for the head, which, in yellow wool with beaks added, or brown-and-white with long ears, could be either chicks or rabbits. I liked the chicken-rabbits, but I still didn't learn to read.

Giles and Mrs Wayne, Betty Evans and Miss Edes (though she was a much more shadowy figure at Westgate than at Headley Down), they were all, to a greater or lesser extent, part of the good side of those eighteen months, the warm, positive, sunlit side. But there was another side, cold, black, negative. There was Miss Axelin, the dark side of the moon, Miss Axelin the Swedish masseuse to whom I went twice a week.

Round the mantelpiece in Miss Axelin's waiting-room there was an embroidered overmantel, white, cold white as the realm of the Snow Queen, on which were worked bears and fir trees and trolls and witches with cauldrons, and little houses deep under snow. Peer Gynt stuff! It fascinated all the many children who went to her, me among the rest. I would be caught up in the fascination, working my way along this overmantel as though it were a strip cartoon, but always with the chill of coming fear at the back of my neck; and then there would be the click of the door opening, and a sense of shadow in the room; and when I turned round, Miss Axelin would be there in her stiff white overall, the little angry red wen burning on the side of her nose, come to take me from my mother and lay me on the high hard white couch in the treatment room.

I don't really know why I was so afraid of her. She hurt me — Swedish massage is fairly gruelling for a seven-year-old — but other people had hurt me, including Mr O'Browne, *dear* Mr O'Browne, whom I had loved. I can only say that I was desperately afraid of her, and so was every child I met who ever came under her shadow. She had, I am sure, religious mania; and her God was an angry God. She was on very close terms with Him, and used to tell us how she had been talking to Him about us and telling Him how wicked we were. But I don't think we were very much afraid of her angry God, just of Miss Axelin herself, who gave off fear as a flower gives off scent. We told lies to please her — no, not to please her, to appease her wrath. At that time, bananas made me sick. She told my mother that I was to have them, mashed with cream and sugar, and I would not be sick unless I was wicked. And then next day in that terrible treatment room, she asked me if I had had a banana. I said yes. She said, 'How many?' and gazing into her implacable face, I abandoned myself to shame. I said only one, but I would have eaten two only Mummy would not give me another. When treatment was over for the day, she led me back to the waiting-room and confronted my mother with having refused me a second banana. My mother never batted an eyelid, she said she considered one banana in a day was enough for one little girl, and had no intention of giving me more. Miss Axelin said, 'You are a wicked woman, and I shall tell God about you and ask Him to punish you!' to which my mother replied that it must be nice to be on such intimate terms with the Almighty, or words to that effect, and swept me off.

We went home in silence, and then, in our little living-room, came the reckoning. My mother did not smack me; but the lash of her tongue was worse. Far worse. I protested wildly and piteously that I had lied because I was afraid. That we were all afraid. That Peter Woods had told Miss Axelin that he had eaten three boiled eggs for breakfast, and they made him sicker than bananas did me ...

In the end, completely by my own decision, and because I needed to make expiation, I wrote and confessed the whole sorry business to my father. I could write a good deal better than I could read. He treasured the letter for many years, and I have seen it often. It had a chalk drawing of a swan on very blue water, surrounded by a garland of violets at the head of the page — I always illustrated my letters to him — and it began:

Dere Darlig Dady, I bin a min snik to Mumy.

My mother, with one of her unexpected and endearing bursts of understanding, made a few enquiries among other mothers and nannies; and I never went back to Miss Axelin again. I believe quite a few other children were taken away from her at the same time.

Anyway, our time at Westgate was beginning to draw to its end. And in an odd sort of way it was beginning to crumble, too. In the spring, along with the primroses and the pink-tipped daisies, Giles's sister Pinkie was born. If she had another name I never heard it, She was so tiny and pink and perfect and good; and slept and smiled and blew bubbles and took her food. (Giles never wanted any food. When he had a birthday cake, he ate the candles, it just didn't make any difference to him.) Mrs Dixon was always looking after her and taking her out in her pram while Giles was left to the maid. There were no more walks together, and the Dent du Leon Farm did not seem the same without Giles and Mrs Dixon.

And then my father came home. I was shy of him as I always was at first, after a long absence. He did not look quite like himself, somehow, until his face had had time to settle down and grow familiar once more. And Westgate, like Malta and Sheerness, opened its doors to let us go, and closed them again behind us.

Giles gave me his Galloping Gus at parting. But we were too young to keep in touch, so we lost each other. For a few years Mrs Dixon and my mother exchanged occasional letters. We heard that Giles was getting steadily better, so much better that he was going to prep school; and then that he had had a relapse; and then we did not hear any more.

I wonder what happened to him?

8

As before, there was a spell in a nursing-home for me, to shut off one chapter from the next, or maybe to make a kind of bridge between them. It was a big nursing-home in Hampstead. I don't remember a thing about the treatment I underwent there; I only know that I was there for six weeks, and that during that time two things happened. One day, two of the nurses, in their free time and bless their kind young hearts, took me to see Queen Mary's Dolls' House; and one night there were strange noises and much coming and going in the eight-bed ward, and I was scared and could not sleep, and the woman in the next bed told me stories and talked to me softly all night long, so that I should not know that at the far end of the ward an older woman was dying, and dying hard.

At the end of the six weeks my parents collected me and took me down to Chatham.

Another dockyard. Another Dockyard Terrace, much bigger than Sheerness. A long row of Georgian houses built on a steep slope so that the gravelled space in front really was a terrace, with a stone balustrade and steps down to the green tree-scattered communal gardens below. The complex of rooms into which the front door opened turned into cellars by the time they reached the back, and the rooms on the ground floor at the back turned into first-floor drawing-rooms by the time they reached the front. Each house had its walled garden, like the Sheerness ones; but to get to it you had to go from the little back yard across a service road and up a long flight of stone steps through a kind of tunnel not unlike Traitor's Gate and just about as inviting.

I had thought at first that now we might have Don back again. But Don was happy with his new family, and

Chatham Dockyard was not really the place for a big dog. It was all so big itself; the yard, the town. No marshes within a few minutes' walk, nothing but streets. It was all right for the Captain's Airedale, Matador Mandarin, because he was a show-dog, Best Dog at Crufts, and was never allowed to walk off the lead anyway, never allowed to run on grass because that would spread his paws, never allowed to get his coat wet. It would have been no life for Don.

I still had my spinal carriage, which now lived in the front porch for afternoon rest sessions only, for I could walk quite well, even, given time, the whole length of the terrace. And I still had my inability to read. My father now joined the battle, and had small serious talks with me.

'When you can read to yourself, old girl, you will find a whole new world opening up to you.'

'Yes, Daddy,' said I. Polite but unconvinced.

He resorted to bribery. I longed to model things. He bought me a box of 'Barbola' modelling clay with all its accompanying paraphernalia, and promised me I should have it when I could read.

'You can't go on like this for *ever!*' he said.

'No, Daddy,' I agreed. I had every intention of going on like it for ever.

'Don't say "No, Daddy".'

'No, Daddy.'

But, at last, help was at hand; somebody told my mother of a little private school in the town. Maybe, if Miss Beck would take me, I might learn better among other children. It was worth trying. Anything was worth trying.

And, oddly enough, I was all for it. I had no real desire to learn to read, but the dignity of schoolgirlhood appealed to me strongly. So there, on a day, was I, my chest swollen with the importance of myself and the occasion, passing for the first time through the doorway of Miss Beck's Academy.

In a small back room with peeling wallpaper, under the eye of a gaunt elderly maid, I was stripped of my coat, leggings and tam-o'-shanter, in company with twelve or fourteen others of my kind. And with them, all on my own, so grown up, I filed through into the schoolroom, to be received, as Royalty receives, by Miss Beck herself, who sat, upright as Royalty sits, in a heavily carved Victorian armchair.

My schooldays proper had begun.

Looking back with warm affection at that first school of mine, I can hardly believe that it was real, and not something dreamed up out of the pages of *Cranford* or *Quality Street*. I suppose nowadays it would not be allowed to exist at all. Miss Amelia Beck had no teaching qualifications whatsoever, save the qualifications of long experience and love. She was the daughter of a colonel of Marines, in her eighty-sixth year when I became one of her pupils; and for more than sixty years, in her narrow house overlooking the Lines at Chatham, she had taught the children of the dockyard and the barracks. She accepted only the children of service families. Oh, the gentle snobbery of a bygone age; bygone even then, and having less to do with class than totem. It was her frequent boast that she had smacked, in their early days, most of the senior officers of both services. Both, not all three, for the RAF was too young as yet to count for much in Miss Beck's scheme of things. But I do not think that it can have been true, unless she had gentled greatly with the passing of the years. For I never knew her to smack anybody during the year that I sat at her feet.

Our school day began with prayers, of the 'Thank you, God, for the lovely world, and please make me a good girl (or boy)' variety ; for which, and for the hymn that followed, we all gathered round Miss Beck at the piano with the green, pleated silk behind its fretwork back.

And, connected with those prayers, I remember vividly a fellow scholar by the name of Micky Porter. Micky was a Roman Catholic and, that being so, his mother asked Miss Beck to excuse him from morning prayers with the rest of us. Micky took this very much amiss, feeling that he was being kept out of something which was therefore, obviously, desirable. But the law was the law; and every day when the polite 'Good mornings' were over, Miss Beck would take him by the hand and lead him ceremoniously to the boxroom, where he was left sitting disconsolate on the black tin uniform case belonging to the late Colonel Beck. Miss Beck would then return to the rest of us, closing the school-room door behind her with a decisive click; and prayers would proceed. Prayers over, she opened the door to go and fetch the exile, and invariably Micky Porter, with his ear to the keyhole, fell into the room. He never learned to remove his ear in time; but Miss Beck never made any comment. Honour, of a sort, had been satisfied and lessons proceeded calmly on their way.

Any elementary schoolteacher of today would have fallen into strong hysterics or sat down with a banner in some public place after one look at our schoolroom, though I don't think we ever had much fault to find with it. It had mud-coloured walls with damp stains in the outer corners, three shelves of limp and weary school-books, a bit of unravelled carpet on the floor. We had no desks; we sat round a vast kitchen table with the initials of long-past admirals and generals carved with illicit pocket-knives among the inkstains on top and down the legs, and we worked our sums and wrote our exercises on slates, with squeaky slate pencils. Some of us ate a good deal of the slate pencils; but myself, I never cared much for the taste. And Miss Beck sat at the head of the table in her carved Victorian chair, with a patchwork cushion made out of crocheted squares, and watched us with a quiet but commanding eye.

We coloured in chalks the elaborate kaleidoscope patterns which she drew for us on our graph paper or with a pair of compasses. We learned deportment, the boys to bow and the girls to curtsey, when we shook hands morning and evening. I, who had stiffened knees and could not curtsey, bowed with the boys; and to this day, I never hand a pair of scissors to anyone without consciously remembering Miss Beck's instructions to do so with the points towards myself and the handle towards the other person. We learned verse upon verse of Macaulay's *Lays of Ancient Rome* and proclaimed them with a glorious fierceness, stiffening the sinews, summoning up the blood and lending the eyes a terrible aspect under the beetling brows of imaginary helmets:

> Lars Porsena of Clusium,
> By the Nine Gods he swore
> That the great house of Tarquin
> Should suffer wrong no more.
> By the Nine Gods he swore it,
> And named a trysting day,
> And bade his messengers ride forth,
> East and West and South and North,
> To summon his array …

Who *were* the Nine Gods? What wrong was the great house of Tarquin suffering? We had no idea. But the lines have the true trumpet ring to them yet; the purposeful tramp of a legion's feet on the march.

From a tattered old volume of Grimm's *Fairy Tales* passed round among us, we learned to read, even I, at long last, discovering suddenly what the mystery was all about. I have no recollection of the actual process; I do not know how or why or when or wherefore the light dawned. I only know that when I went to Miss Beck's Academy I could not read, and that by the end of my first term, without any apparent transition period, I was reading, without too much trouble, anything that came my way.

We had no regular 'break' in the midst of all this cerebral activity. Instead, we were allowed five minutes off whenever Miss Beck thought fit, to crowd the window and lean our stomachs on the sill and admire the Beauties of Nature. The chestnut trees along the road breaking into leaf, a rainbow, a dog playing with a ball, soldiers drilling on the Lines, to Miss Beck they all counted as Beauties of Nature. And, our five minutes being up, we were recalled to our places and our lessons again, until the next Beauty of Nature should happen along.

As to our places, there was very little dividing into age groups; the slightly older of us sat with the slightly younger in our midst, and did our best to keep them in order and teach them the usages of civilised society which we ourselves had acquired. My own especial charge was a red-haired imp called Alexander (Sandy, he would not have), who smiled like a small seraph above the table and kicked like a mule under it. And I remember so well Susan Tonks, of the straight black hair and sweetly serious blue eyes, gravely trying to teach a particularly unpleasant little boy, who shall be nameless because he grew up to follow his father into the Marines and marry and become all that he should, how to blow his nose instead of picking it or letting it run.

It was the start of the Easter term when I first entered Miss Beck's small enclosed world, and in the course of many five-minute breaks, I saw the buds thicken on the trees, and the March rainbows, and the pink chestnut blossom fall, or the blue smoke of bonfires on the Lines burning autumn leaves.

As Christmas term drew on, we began to be very busy

making things. My mother possessed for many years the Union Jack cross-stitch kettle-holder which I made for her at that time. We sang carols round the green-pleated-silk piano, with candles glimmering in the brass candleholders, in honour of Christmas time, as the dark of the year drew in. 'Away in a Manger' we sang, and 'The First Noel', and 'Once in Royal David's City', and the excitement shimmered brighter as the last days of the term went by; and the whole house, schoolroom and all, began to submerge under a drift of Christmas cards that piled up on every ledge and came fluttering down from their perches every time anybody opened or shut a door.

Christmas cards from old boys in big ships of the China Station and dusty cantonments on the plains of India; from fishery protection gunboats tossing in the North Sea; from Camberley and Greenwich and the Persian Gulf. Christmas cards from old girls in married quarters and rooms and small rented houses up and down the world, usually enclosing letters and snapshots and messages of love from small sons and daughters whom Miss Beck had never seen. Miss Beck's old pupils seldom forgot her, and woe betide any of them who did. 'I have not heard from Elaine this year. Of course her mother was always unsatisfactory, and they allowed her to use face powder much too young. I shall write to her in the New Year.' Or, 'I must say, I did not think Peter would have forgotten me so soon. He was a very affectionate little boy. I suppose getting his regiment so young has gone to his head.'

On the last day of all, we had a party. The battered kitchen table blossomed into iced cakes and jellies; and when the feast was over, Miss Beck disappeared into her bedroom and came back again wearing her best black velvet hat, and a wonderful old paisley shawl the colour of violets and fading rose-petals, and announced that she was the Duchess of Devonshire and had come to present the prizes!

There was a prize for everybody, so that nobody should have hurt feelings. Not prizes for any particular subject, just prizes. Mine, almost the only school prize I ever won, was *The Cuckoo Clock* and I have it still.

After we left Chatham, Miss Beck and I wrote to each other until I was quite grown up and she had long since retired, for she lived into her late nineties. And then the time came when I wrote as usual, and there was no answer to my letter, and no answer to the next letter either. And I knew, even before I wrote to the old housemaid to ask for news, that all of us, scattered over the face of the earth like Kipling's Slaves of the Lamp, had lost our Miss Amelia Beck, and a tiny part of our own lives with her.

9

The front doors of all the Chatham Dockyard houses opened straight into long dark rooms, each running the whole width of its house, and with a fairly imposing staircase leading up to the house proper. Some of these front rooms had names, bestowed on them long since and passed on from generation to generation of the people who had lived in the houses for a year or two and then passed on their way. One was called Grandmother's Tomb; ours was called the Bar Parlour. What purpose they can have originally been intended for, Heaven alone knows. One or two of them were used as billiard rooms, but in most cases they were handed over to the children, when there were children to hand them over to. And we lived our young social lives in the gloomy splendour of each other's Bar Parlours or to and fro along the terrace outside.

For no matter how inferior Chatham was to Sheerness in most ways — all those dark streets, and no country to be got at save by car on special occasions, and the fact that Sheerness had always been, for the adult population, a 'happy' yard, whereas Chatham was an 'unhappy' one, torn with small social feuds and jealousies — to me it had one priceless advantage. There were other children round about my own age. Not only the children I met daily at Miss Beck's Academy when I started going to school, but children dotted all along the terrace.

There was Yvonne O'Neil, the Captain's daughter. She was two years older than me, and pulled seniority at times, a pretty, affected little girl who had been sent to a convent school in Switzerland as a cure for asthma and had what Jean (I will come to Jean later) and I considered Silly French Ways in consequence. She was always being somebody else. ▸

'Now I am Marie Antoinette,' she would announce, draping the tablecloth over her head. 'See how proudly I walk to the guillotine.' But most often, she was Mary Queen of Scots. I once got let in for being all four of the other Marys, while she acted a long play which she had made up about that most boring of queens all one afternoon.

There were the King boys next door, who went to the grammar school and were kindly, though rather above my head, and had a little dog called Lulu, for whose affections they quite frequently fought. My mother once invited them in to help pick the mulberries from the tree in our garden. On the first day their mother sent them in immaculate cricketing flannels. The youngest actually sat in a basket of mulberries: the other two were not quite so thorough, but not, as it were, far behind. And the next day they came to finish the job in bathing trunks.

There was Michael Pallot in the holidays, eleven years old and lordly from his prep school, who climbed the garden wall to teach me Latin whether I would or no. I didn't really want to learn Latin, even

> Amo, amas, I loved a lass, and she was tall and slender,
> Amas, Amat, I knocked her flat, and broke her teeth on
> the fender.

I didn't really much like Michael Pallot. But I hated being alone in that garden; the steps and the tunnel and the road between it and the house made it as lonely as a desert island, but without the exciting possibilities. So I welcomed his coming with slightly more warmth than I would otherwise have done.

There were Doodie and Pixie from the far end of the terrace. What their real names were, I have no idea. Pixie deserved something better, being quite a pleasant if nondescript five-year-old. But Doodie aged seven was an obnoxious little boy, swollen-headed, silly, and a bully to boot. He had a tin sword, which some misguided person had made for him. I had a wooden sword, much treasured. My father had bound the hilt with string, like the grip of a real sword, and painted it gold. The gold came off in my small hot hand, but I loved it none the less for that. Doodie got me cornered one day, his tin sword to my wooden one. It was a somewhat uneven fight, and I was driven back to the wall, Doodie executing a kind of triumph dance in front of me, shouting, 'I've won, Rosemary! I've won!' The battle fury of all the heroes of all the books my mother had read me swelled in my bosom, and nerved my arm. 'Yes, you've won, Doodie,' I shouted back, 'but I'm not beaten yet!' and fetched him a final thwack with Excalibur.

Alas, it did not split his head open, it did not even leave a scratch; and I have a horrible feeling that the story would have had an ignominious end had not some adult appeared on the scene, causing Doodie to withdraw rather hurriedly. My mother, who believed in letting things take their course, and had heard the exchange from the drawing-room window above, was suddenly and unexpectedly proud of me, and showed me her family crest on a silver spoon; a wolf bleeding from the mouth, and under it the motto, 'Laesus non victus' and told my father when he came home. It was all very pleasant at first, but rather puzzling. And then there began to be a faint dismay.

As I have said before, disabled children often have an odd unawareness or only partial awareness of how it is with them. They know that they cannot do certain things which other children can do. They know, as it were, in theory, but they have not yet got the full impact. Soon, all too soon, they become aware of subtle social barriers, the full implication and likely effect on their lives, the loneliness. But at nine or ten many handicapped children, myself amongst them, are at the stage at which I put Drem, when I came to write *Warrior Scarlet* thirty years later. Drem, who knew that he could not use his right arm, but had never considered the possibility that it could in any way prevent him from taking his place among the warriors of his tribe.

So I did not really understand that my mother's real pride in me was because I had taken on the non-handicapped world on equal terms (not even equal, my sword wasn't tin!) and if not beaten it at its own game, at least refused to accept defeat. I did not suffer any sudden and shattering realisation, even then; but none the less, it was the beginning; and Doodie was the cause of it; and I did not love Doodie ...

There was Sheila Walker who was six, and who, I am ashamed to say, Jean and I used to terrorize. She did ask for it — she grizzled and told tales — but still, we should not have fed her on dandelion leaves and then told her they were deadly poison. I see that now. At the time, it seemed like a good idea.

Above all, there was Jean Noble, who lived next door on the other side.

I have no recollection of our first meeting, but I never remember a time at Chatham when we were not 'best friends'. It was the first time I had ever had a 'best friend'. Giles was something quite different. Jean and I giggled in corners, and told each other things which were deadly secrets from all the rest of the world. She was plump and pretty and pink as a full-blown rose, not to say beefy; which was sad, because she had ambitions to be one of those elfin children, all bird bones and enormous eyes, beneath whose feet the grass scarcely bends. Alas, her legs were sturdy and her feet came down with a resounding plonk at every step, no matter how she tried. She had a sister, Ruth, and a brother, Alan, but both were so much older than her that the long front room of her house was as exclusively hers as mine was mine; and after school — the Grammar School in her case — and in the holidays, we seemed to spend most of our time in and out of each other's territory. Hers was rather superior to mine, having curtains and flowery wallpaper; though whether that was her family's doing — a Grannie and an Auntie as well as mother and father, brother and sister, were all part of the household — or had merely been inherited from previous inhabitants I do not know. What I do know is that her doll's house, which was also prettier than mine, was definitely the doing of her father and Alan.

Oh, how I envied her that doll's house! Mine, made for me by one of the dockyard shipwrights to my father's specification, was beautifully sound and serviceable, but not pretty at all. It was very square, with putty-coloured walls and a red roof ruled off with lines of white paint to indicate tiles, its interior painted hospital green throughout. Though not usually lacking in imagination, I never realised what marvels could have been wrought with a lick of prettier paint and a few scraps of wallpaper. Perhaps I thought my family would be hurt or cross if I did not like it just as it was. Perhaps I did not really feel that it was mine, to the extent of such major alterations. I don't know.

But Jean's doll's house! She had the advantage, of course, that her father was not actually a sailor at all, but a Naval Constructor, (as Jean, in one of our occasional tiffs, once said to me, 'My father builds the ships. Yours only makes them go!') and he could build, make, construct other things than ships. With the help of Alan, surely the nicest of all elder brothers, he had conjured up a dream of delight. White walls, a roof of many steep gables covered with big round tiles — the waxed card milk-bottle tops of those days — lacquered ruby red and gloriously shiny; diamond-paned windows and sprigged wallpaper; muslin curtains made by Grannie and Auntie, in one window a tiny yellow canary in a cage; and, glory of glories, electric light that really worked — Alan joined the electrical branch of the Navy and was killed in 1941.

In other ways, too, Mr Noble was a constructor. At Christmas, he constructed us a pantomime, a gorgeous *mélange* of *Aladdin* combined with bits and pieces of any other pantomime that occurred to him as he went along, including *Jack and the Beanstalk*. Jean played Jack, and I, joy of joys, played Jill. There was, come to think of it, no Aladdin at all; but Mr Noble himself played Wicked Uncle Ebenaza, while Ruth descended from the dignity of her sixteen years to play almost everybody else. We performed it, of course, in the long front room, with curtains rigged up on a clothes line across the end where the stairs went up; the Forest, which was our chief scene, was made by tying branches of evergreens to the banisters. Costumes were no problem, as Jean had a 'dress-up box' containing, among other splendours, a yellow dust-sheet for Ebenaza's cloak, and a slightly careworn white ballet skirt for the Good Fairy. Alan declined to take part, but became our effects man, and produced, among other things, a most realistic thunderstorm, at the height of which, Uncle Ebenaza was magicked into the Nobles' marmalade cat. (Deafening applause from the audience, consisting of my parents and Jean's mother, Grannie and Auntie.) The two lines which followed the metamorphosis, I am still word perfect in.

'Come on,' said Jack, clutching the startled and struggling animal, 'let's throw him in the river!' To which I replied, as well as I could for giggles, 'No, Jack, be kind and give him liver.'

Jean and I had, as I think a great many best friends have, a secret make-believe world of our own. We had only to say, 'Let's be Lilian and Diana', and, as though it was a magical formula, step straight into a world that was as real to us as the world of school and parents and cornflakes for breakfast. It was a boarding-school world — nothing very unusual or original in that — based heavily on the writings of Angela Brazil and *The Schoolgirl's Own* — my father had been right when he said that learning to read would open up a whole new world to me! — in which Jean-become-Lilian was inclined to be noble (no play on names intended) while I, as Diana, was more the 'tomboy of the IVth' type. Together we got involved in terrible school adventures, stood up to unjust mistresses, bore the most hideous punishments rather than sneak, and in all kinds of adversity stood by each other to the last steps of Caesar's throne, until the everyday world in one form or another, probably supper, called us away. Then we would simply lay down the endless serial at whatever stage in the current crisis had been reached until next day, when we would pick it up again exactly where we had left off. 'Let's be Lilian and Diana ...'

In the summer after my father retired, Jean came to stay with me in North Devon. On the first morning, we retired to the rustic summerhouse. 'Let's be Lilian and Diana ...'

But the magic formula no longer worked. We tried and tried; but one could only act Lilian and Diana; we could not be them any more. I suppose the break had been too long, and we were just too old. We went on trying for days, searching for the way in. But it was like searching for the lost door to a lost country. Finally, without anything actually being said between us, we gave up and turned to other things. But with Lilian and Diana, something of Jean and Rosemary had gone too; left behind the lost door to the lost country. It was one of the saddest experiences of my young life.

10

During our time at Chatham I heard a great deal of mention, at adult level, of 'the Zone'. My father was in the Zone, the time when one does, or does not, get promotion. And it must have been an anxious time for him, and for my mother; and then a sad time, for he did not get his Fourth Stripe, or rather he only got it on the day before he retired, according to the rather cruel custom of Their Lordships of the Admiralty. Promotion is a chancy thing and can depend on so many chances; on being in the right place at the right time, even on making oneself pleasant to the right woman, or playing a good game of tennis, as well as being a good officer. It shouldn't be that way, but it was; still is, for all I know. My father's great grief was that he had never commanded his own ship. That, too, is something of a matter of chance; a Lieutenant or Lieutenant Commander may command a small ship, but it so happened that my father's postings, after his very young days, were all to big ships. So, at forty-four years old, here was the end — until the Second World War called him back again eight years later — to his life with the Navy. And, as was the case with most sailors in his day, not perhaps quite so much now in these days of short-term commissions and the like, the Navy was his life.

I realised something of this, and felt drawn to him, partly in sympathy, but also, I think, because we had reached the natural time to begin drawing towards each other.

Until Chatham, my mother had been the central point of all things for me, the one who was always there. My father was on the edge; there in patches and away in longer patches. Also, we had very little in common until that time. I have noticed the same thing with other naval officers and their children. Again, it is different now, when service families are far less separated than they were when I counted my age in single figures. Fathers were away so much then that every time they came back they and their children were strangers to each other, and had to get to know each other all over again. And I think, too, that quite often — I am sure unconsciously — the father would resent, just a little, the claims of almost unknown children on the woman he loved and did not want to share. But when the children began to be companionable, people in their own right, possible helpers in hobbies and sharers of interests, then it was quite a different matter. There is no nicer and more satisfactory father than the sailor home from the sea. 'I think Daddy rather likes me, now that I'm useful to him,' said one eleven-year-old of my acquaintance years later.

It was beginning to be like that between my father and me. We became real to each other for the first time. I must always have been a very great anxiety to him, but that is another kind of reality. My first real memories of him as a person date from around that time. I remember having a birthday, and being allowed not only to sit up to supper, but to invite Jean to join me. How pretty my mother made the table, with candles and her cherished Limerick lace mats, and little paper cups of sugared almonds beside each place; and how perfectly my father played the host, with the grave courtesy which later endeared him to many children; and how, after supper, with the gramophone playing 'The Blue Danube', he danced with both of us, one at a time, I mean, with our feet planted on his, which must have been uncomfortable to say the least of it, but which Jean and I both found delightful.

My father tried to initiate me into the joys and mysteries of astronomy. Not astronomer's astronomy, but seaman's astronomy. Being an executive officer, a navigator, what is now called Seaman Branch, he knew the night skies like his own back yard. Alas, I never learned to do more than find and identify with some difficulty the Pole Star, Venus and Jupiter and the Great Bear. Orion was easier, with his narrow waist cinched in with stars, his striding legs and swaggering shoulders, his sword and his two dogs — two, for Procyon comes closer to his heel than Sirius whom everybody knows. Oh, but the names of those stars and constellations, names familiar from my earliest days, out of Greek-Roman myth, names from the Arabic and yet stranger tongues; Andromeda and Pegasus and the Pleiades, Betelgeuse and Bellatrix and Aldebaran; they sang themselves over in my mind, making strong magic, never, unfortunately, making sense.

What made much more sense were the photograph albums which he and I would explore together. Brown hessian covers to be folded back with a heart-leap of expectancy, the same expectancy every time. And inside, coming up to meet me from the thick brown pages, photographs, almost new, or beginning to be faded and yellowed by time, mostly with captions in white ink underneath in my father's neat hand. Photographs of ships, HMS *Proserpine*, HMS *Pathfinder*. Ship's dogs, ship's cats, the assembled casts of ship's productions of *The Mikado*, ship's cricket elevens. Of grinning faces in balaclava helmets, with icebergs in the background. 'Brownger, Kennedy, Ross and self. White Sea, '07' the caption would read. And 'He was one of our Snotties in the *Bacchante*,' my father would say, indicating a young man in tropical whites, with Table Mountain in the background and yet another ship's cat in his arms. 'Went down at Jutland.'

Best of all were the pictures of places. Pompeii, with the wheel ruts of chariots deeply shadowed by the afternoon sun on a paved street; a view over mountain-rides of Burmese tea estates; royal elephants in the forecourt of a rajah's palace; sailing ships in Table Bay, Bahrain and Kuwait and such-like ports and principalities of the Persian Gulf — oil kingdoms now, but huddles of mud houses amid baking desert when those photographs were taken, and the local sheikh posing for the photograph with his curved dagger in his belt and his favourite falcon on his fist or his eldest son at his knee; or a British Resident wearing a topee and riding a camel. Greece, above all, with the Lion Gate at Mycenae in the days when you could pick up shards of Mycenaean pottery as easily as anemones from the rough grass. Those yellowing photos of the Lion Gate, even more than the classical myths on which I had been brought up, first declared Greece unto me, and gave me the hunger for Hellenic soil and clear light and wind-silvered olive trees, and the sense of home-coming which was waiting for me when at last I actually got there, and has greeted me on each return ever since.

My father was no story-teller in the accepted sense of the word; not as my mother was a story-teller; not even as my Uncle Harold. But listening to him as he chatted of this and that, turning the familiar pages, I gathered a good many stories all the same. Of the war between two Persian Gulf sheikhdoms (I *think* it was Shah-Ja and Abu Musa, but would not like, at this distance of time, to be dogmatic), which went on for years, punctuated by courteous periods of truce while both sides returned each other's cherished stone cannonballs, and the daily ceasefire while the Resident took his afternoon ride. Of the struggle between two of HM ships of China Station for possession of a brass dragon-shaped cannon captured in the Boxer Rising. Of the penguins of Baffin Island who used to come aboard to warm themselves at the galley fire; and the Gurkha officers who would come to dinner in the wardroom, caring nothing, apparently, for the laws that bind all other caste Hindus. Of the men of the Transjordanian Camel Corps who, on the other hand, would get up with perfect courtesy and good temper and empty their food-bowls into the sand because some careless white man and unbeliever had let his shadow fall across them. Stories from another world long since lost. Useful bits of advice and information from another world, too: that the best omelettes and black figs in Greece were to be got from the attendant of the hot baths at Thermai, on the island of Samos; that when dealing with a *dhow* suspected of gun-running you should never come up to board her on the leeward side, unless you wanted her to drop her lateen sail on top of you and get away while you floundered.

What was he like, my father? A short, stockily-built man — a countryman's build with shoulders that looked deceptively sloping because of the development of muscle out from the base of the neck. He had the springy walk that comes partly from being bred in a hilly country — for though one could not describe North Devon as mountainous, most of it slopes sharply up or down — partly from being used to marching. My mother once said that when you saw my father walking, you expected to hear the band. You could never, for a moment, have mistaken him for anything but a sailor. He had a quiet, steady face with a cleft chin, and grey-blue eyes crinkled up by the years of narrowing them against rain and wind — ships did not have their bridges glassed in in his day. He had the spectacularly bushy eyebrows so often possessed by seamen. I have often wondered whether God, knowing that they are going to sea and will need such protection, endows them with the ability to grow such eyebrows at the moment of conception, or whether they grow them simply out of need, as one develops a suntan or a callus, when the time comes. He had a dark beard, or would have had, if he had grown it, and this, combined with the mass of tiny wind-broken veins, gave him a face reddish and weatherbeaten to look at, harsh to the touch. But by Chatham days I had already made the discovery that his temples and the wrinkled skin round his eyes were incredibly soft and silky to my fingertips, and that the lobes of his ears were like velvet.

He was a quiet man, as the husbands of volatile women so often are, quiet also in the way that some sailors are. There seems to be a widely-held belief among the non-naval population that all naval officers are the life and soul of every party they go near, that they drink pink gin in large quantities, and cast the glad eye, if nothing more, at every woman in sight. This may be true of a certain section; but there is another, a quiet section, interested only in their own wives, and not much interested in gin at all. My father belonged very definitely to this section, and so did most of the men who were his friends. Sticky, worthy, dull, I suppose. He didn't even swear beyond an occasional 'damn'. 'If you swear at your men, they get used to it, and you've nothing left in reserve to make them jump with when you really need to.' Not what the world of the uninitiated considers a typical sailor. But he was typical of his kind. A simple man, hopelessly lacking in any imagination — but my mother had enough for both halves of any marriage — with a strong faith in his own unorthodox God, born, I think, of long solitary hours on watch, and the great loneliness of sky and waters.

Most sailors keep a lot of their youth about them always. Grey-haired and dripping with gold lace, they will climb through the backs of wardroom chairs on guest nights. And many of them retain, all their lives, a surprising gift for hero-worship. For Nelson, of course; but also for personal heroes of their own. My father's was Sir Christopher Cradock, who went down at Coronel in 1914. My father was his pilot, and would have gone down with him but for a last-minute transfer. Sir Christopher Cradock wore steel-boned corsets and used scent. He used regularly to arrive on the bridge when my father was bringing the ship into harbour, and say, 'Thirty seconds late, Pilot,' to which my father would reply, 'Sir, kindly get off my bridge, you are upsetting my compass.' Years later, when I came to know about such things, I said to my father, 'Was he a homosexual?' My father looked at me with clear surprised eyes, and said, 'No, just Elizabethan like Drake and Raleigh.' At all events, whether Sir Christopher was gay, or just three hundred years out of his time, he had it in him to inspire hero-worship in one young navigating officer that lasted him the rest of his life.

So — my father 'retired with the rank of Captain'.

And my mother, watching him take off his uniform for the last time, said, 'It's all right; you'll be putting that on again before ten years are up.' She was given to what she claimed were flashes of the Second Sight. They did not always come true, but sometimes they did. Eight years later, just two days before the outbreak of the Second World War, my father was back in uniform again. And this time he got his command of a ship, more than one, wildly and hilariously assorted ships, before peace broke out again.

11

We were leaving one world and moving on to another. In one way we were moving back, to the world that had been my father's before the sea. For after toying with the idea of going to live in South Africa, it was decided that we should go back to North Devon and find a home where he had been born and bred.

He had never lost touch with his roots, and neither had we, for always, when leave was long enough to make the journey worthwhile, we had headed back for Torrington on its high gorse-grown common above the Torridge, to stay with Mrs Penhorwood who had been cook at the Big House when he was a boy, and was now widow of the local butcher and let rooms, but only to the chosen few and on personal recommendation.

Mrs Penhorwood was little and bent, and her breakfasts were things to dream about: grilled kidneys dripping red onto their toast, crisp curled bacon and fluffy scrambled egg and creamy chicken croquettes — not on separate days, but all at the same time!

She had a grandfather clock with the sun and moon on its face, and a painted galleon beneath them, which rocked to and fro as the seconds passed: 'Tick-tock, Tick-tock.' There was a stuffed fox that lived on top of the wardrobe in the room where I slept, keeping watch over me with a cold glass eye through the night; and a yew tree outside my window that had a witch's profile, and gave me delightful shivers. Above all, she had cockcrow. I do not mean that she had a cock; I don't think she kept poultry. But her house was on the edge of the little market town, and beyond it was farmland, and the crowing of a cock in the green first-light of my first morning, every first morning of every leave we spent there, was part of Mrs Penhorwood to me. On later mornings it would be a nice sound, but not especially magical. But in that first dawn it would fall on my town-dulled ears as something very magical indeed, something to shiver at with delight and something stranger than mere delight. It was the perfect sound to enter through magic casements opening wide on perilous seas and fairylands forlorn. It was a sound with a bloom on it, like dew, and shaped like a fleur-de-lys. To this day, the sound of a cock crowing in the early morning, though one seldom hears it in this world of battery hens, is magical to me; an incredibly lonely sound, pricking the dawn with that sharp centre petalpoint-spearpoint of a fleur-de-lys. But to hear the bloom on it, you must be just back in the country, with your ears newly awakened from a long spell in town.

I cannot remember that we ever *did* anything during those leaves. We just *were*. Except that one day I went fishing with my father in the Torridge. There we were, among the purple loosestrife and the alder scrub, while my mother sat reading under a nearby tree; he with his long lithe rod and whirring reel and the little feathery fly dancing on the water, I with my safety-pin on the end of a piece of string on the end of a stick. He caught a trout. Probably he caught more than one; but I only remember the first, lying on the bank, beautiful with the rose flecks on its sides that faded a little as time went by. But I caught nothing. I must have been very young and trusting, because it never occurred to me until long after, when I was at least seven, that the reason I did not catch anything was that my safety-pin was closed. Oh, the perfidy of adults!

But all that was long ago when we came to stay with Mrs Penhorwood while we looked for a house to live in — slightly hampered in our efforts by the kind offices of old

Mrs Thurgood. Mrs Thurgood was immensely fat, and much given to bridge coats made from wonderful old materials, brocades and cut velvets, which she dug out of chests in the attic. She sat all day long in a high-backed, carved, oak chair in the bow window of her little house in South Street; the window opened directly onto the pavement, and Mrs Thurgood sat there like a fat benevolent spider, happy in the knowledge that everybody she knew — and she knew everybody in Torrington — would have to pass within six inches of her as they went about their shopping and other daily business. Then Mrs Thurgood would rap on the window and nod and beckon. 'Come in, my dear, du'ee come in!' Mrs Thurgood's father had fifteen quarterings on his coat-of-arms; her mother had been a pretty girl from the local glove factory; and the brocades and cut velvets of her bridge jackets came from her father's world, while her accent came from her mother's, the broadest and softest of Devonshire burrs. 'Du'ee come in, my dear zoul,' Mrs Thurgood would command rather than invite. And if some hard-pressed friend, desperate to get home to lunch or pick up the children from school or simply not to get caught, pretended not to see or hear, Mrs Thurgood would send one of her two pretty maids — she always had two maids, and they always had to be pretty, it was so well known that plain girls never even applied — running after them with the message, 'Please, Mrs Thurgood says you'm to come in for a tell.' If people were *really* desperate for time, they went round by back streets, three times as far, but quicker in the long run.

Mrs Thurgood had been a friend of my grandparents; she had known my father all his life, and thoroughly approved of my mother. So as soon as she knew that we were in need of a home, she started thinking. 'I've been thinking,' she would say. 'Little Silver would suit'ee proper,' or 'Thicky ol' vicarage over to Black Torrington might be just what you'm looking for.'

'Is Mrs Tod selling, then?' my father would enquire.

'How should I know? But no harm in asking. Du'ee go and ask'en, my dear.'

She would have sent him round asking the owners of most of the nice houses in North Devon if they were selling, if she had had her way.

In the end we found our own home for our own selves. We found Netherne, which was to be home to us for more than twenty years.

It was quite an ordinary sort of house, with white rough-cast walls and a red roof; but its ex-teaplanter owner, who now wanted the gentler climate of South Devon, had built on a kind of glassed-in verandah running the full length of the front of the house. Known as the 'Stoep' in his day and in ours, this made a lovely spacious dayroom and gave the house a roominess it would not otherwise have had, though we later found that it was hell to keep warm in the winter. There were outbuildings too, a great draw, as my father, like many of his kind, was set on keeping chickens. But the thing that made the house like no other house was its position.

It was closely related to Wuthering Heights, perched up on the high ground, moor and hill-farm country, between the Taw and the Torridge. Three big fields went with the house, and a three-acre spinney surrounded it on two and a half sides, without whose shelter it would surely have blown away altogether on the wings of the westerly gales that made the trees grow all one way and salt-burned their leaves to brown before ever the colours of autumn came. From the upstairs windows you could look out to Exmoor in one direction and the dim blue shape of Dartmoor in another; and the only reason you could not cover Bideford Bay to

Lundy in a third was because the sheltering arm of the little wood came between.

Bideford was six miles away, Barnstaple eight, Torrington nearly four. Even Yarnscombe, the tiny dropped-off-the-end-of-the-world village which was 'ours' was more than two. And there we sat, in the middle of nowhere.

'It's lovely, but isn't it dreadfully lonely in the winter?' said summer-visiting relations. 'Not a bit — you're never lonely in the country,' we said. As the years went by, I personally began to be a little less sure of that. But from the first year to the last, I loved Netherne, even when I did find it lonely. I loved my small bedroom, one window looking to Dartmoor, the other straight into the crown of a big lilac tree and across that, down the length of the kitchen garden, to the wood. I loved going to bed on winter nights with Orion hanging in at the Dartmoor window, getting up on winter mornings to fifty miles of flaming sunrise. I loved the curlews coming up from the coast in March to breed on the rough fields around the house — March nights when their calling, that wonderful ascending spiral of sound which is their full mating call, went on till midnight and started again four hours later. I still miss the curlews, and the fifty-mile sunsets and sunrises, and the fox-gloves in the deep-banked Devon lanes in June. I think I always will.

By that first summer we were settled in. The hens were in residence; and in a sort of cabin in the garden, my father was writing Sailing Directions for the Admiralty, a job which goes on ceaselessly, each volume being out of date and in need of rewriting almost as soon as it is published. That was the summer when Jean came to stay; the sad visit on which we failed to find our way back into the world of Lilian and Diana. Jean left the bath-tap running undiscovered for a couple of hours, which did not endear her to my father who had pumped the water up from the well to the tank in the roof (we had a donkey engine to do it later), and altogether the visit was not without its dramas and disasters. We shared the spare room and sat up in bed talking till all hours, or what seemed to us all hours, despite visits from my mother telling us to lie down and go to sleep. And we had picnics at Westward Ho! and we made a 'den' for ourselves in the old rickety summerhouse and told ourselves we felt ever so cosy in it. But nothing was quite what it had been; and before the next summer Jean and her family had gone to Scotland, so there were no more visits.

Still, we have never quite lost touch, though nowadays it is a letter at Christmas. I must ask her, one day, whether she remembers Lilian and Diana.

We had a dog again; Mike, an Airedale puppy. He was own son to Matador Mandarin of Chatham Dockyard days, but with no pretensions to being a show-dog like his father. My father did enter him for a puppy show at Bridgwater, and he won a third in his class and a silver cup the size of a thimble, on which my father proudly had his name engraved. It has long since lost its black bakelite stand and one handle, but it still makes the ideal vase for the very tiniest winter nosegays, little crumpled violets and winter cyclamen and half-inch sprigs of rosemary. But after that he and my father agreed that the life of a show-dog was not for him; so he lived the life of a country gentleman, and knew all the joys of running free and rabbiting that were denied to Matador.

When he was about a year old, Don came back to us. His family were moving, and would have no room for him any more. He came back to us old and fat and half-blind; and we were all worried as to how Mike would receive him. We need not have had a single qualm. My father met him at the station and brought him home. He had travelled by himself in a muzzle and a label saying, 'If I pant, please give me a drink'. But the guard, an enlightened soul, had removed the muzzle before they were well clear of Waterloo, and they arrived bosom friends. The car drew up, the door opened, and Don bumbled stiffly out. Mike, waiting with my mother and me, advanced and smelled him very carefully all over, and quite clearly said, 'My eye! You are out of condition, aren't you, old chap? Never mind, we'll soon cure that.' They then, with due ceremony, watered the same clump of tulips by the front door, and departed as though they had known each other all their lives to look for a rat in one of the out-houses.

For six months they were inseparable. They hunted together, returning home leg-weary, muddied to the eyebrows, and blissfully happy. If Don did not at first want to come, Mike would get him by the collar and firmly haul him out. But after a time this ceased to be necessary. The years and the fat rolled off the old hero, giving him a new lease of life.

Alas, it was not a very long lease. After six months he had a fit, and then a worse one. My father took him to the vet, and brought his tired old body back; and we buried him in the wood, just outside the garden gate, where he had loved to lie because it was one of those natural vantage points from which a dog can see all that is going on. We all cried. And Mike was bewildered and inconsolable. For days he hunted the house and garden, the out-buildings and the country round. For months, after he had really given up the search, he would get sudden ideas: 'Of course! That's where he is! Why didn't I think of that before?' and go jauntily off to look in some place where he had looked fifty times already; and come back with his tail down and ears drooping, going to my father for comfort and if possible, please, the easing of the bewilderment inside him.

Privately, we suspected that it was his efforts to rejuvenate him that had worn Don out, but at any rate the old dog's last six months had been very happy ones.

At the beginning of that first summer term, almost before we had settled into our new home, and just about the time Mike joined the family, I started school again.

St George's School. Private and PNEU, but very much larger than Miss Beck's Academy. We wore panama hats with red-and-white ribbon round them, and were expected to behave ourselves in the street in a way which would not bring dishonour upon the school, the United Kingdom including Church and Crown, or the British Empire. Beside Miss Davies the Headmistress, there was an assistant who took the juniors in another classroom, and various visiting staff including Miss Wright who taught us music and the curate who taught us Latin. He used to stride up and down the aisle between the desks, lightly rapping people on the head with the Latin grammar when they got it wrong. I almost invariably got it wrong. I got most things wrong. I did not do nearly as well in any direction at St George's as I had done at Miss Beck's. It was mostly my own fault; Miss Davies was a nice, conscientious, well-meaning woman and a properly qualified teacher; but she lacked the natural gift for teaching that Miss Beck had, and she had something that raised the devil in me. King Charles's Head.

She was a devout high churchwoman and tried hard to make us over in her own image, though without much success. Most of us were Wesleyan or United Methodist; I had been brought up in the lowest possible layer of the Church of England. She was an ardent Royalist in the Stuart sense of the word, and all roads led quite literally to King Charles's Head; not only the roads of history lessons, but religious tuition, even geography. I don't think she ever quite managed it with maths, but I am sure she would have if she could. I, on the other hand, had been brought up ardently Cromwellian by an ardently Cromwellian mother, and this did not make for harmony between us. Most of the school followed her lead in the matter of King Charles's Head quite happily, and turned up wearing sprigs of oak leaves on Oak Apple Day, but a boy called Michael Vincent and I formed a two-man Cromwellian faction in an otherwise Royalist school, and very much enjoyed being an oppressed and rebellious minority. It was fun, but it didn't really get one anywhere. It certainly didn't get me anywhere, and somewhere along the way Miss Davies lost me all interest in learning anything at all. It wasn't all her fault, far the larger share must have been mine, but it was partly her doing, all the same.

Maybe it was the wrong sort of school for me; though at least we were a cross-section of society, this time, which must have broadened my outlook for me. I have always been thankful that at any rate it was not a 'special' school, not that I think there were many, in those days. Some special schools are special in a rather different way; I know of one, catering for severely handicapped boys who are mentally above normal, which is very definitely special for the high level of intelligence as well as for the handicap. Ordinary special schools are of course necessary in certain cases, especially if the handicap be mental, or in the case of a deaf or blind child. But if it can be managed in any way, no child, I believe, should go to a special school who can possibly cope and be coped with in a normal one. A handicapped child who is going to grow up and live his or her life in the world of the unhandicapped will do so far more confidently and naturally if he shares the same school from an early age than if he emerges suddenly in his late teens from the sheltered and specialised environment into an open world which is strange to him.

People — parents — are sometimes worried about the kind of treatment a disabled child will receive at the hands of his 'whole' schoolmates. Will he be actually bullied or terrorised? Will the other children say cruel things? Make him feel an outcast? The inhumanity of child to child is well known, and the law of the jungle, whereby the pack turns on the outsider, the weakling. I can only say, with deep thankfulness, that nothing of that sort ever came my way at school. The other children at St George's, as at Miss Beck's, took me in their stride. and save for an occasional kindly 'Can you manage?' or the alteration in the rules of some game during break, so that I could take part in it, they never seemed particularly aware of any difference between us. I was simply one of themselves who happened not to be able to walk very well.

The only time I ever suffered the experience of the pack turning on the outsider, it was at the hands of my own kind, in hospital; and that was for a very different reason.

12

For the next few years hospital alternated with school as my point of contact with other children. I departed at intervals, eight or ten times it must have been, to the Princess Elizabeth Orthopaedic Hospital in Exeter for operations that attempted with varying success to repair the damage left by Still's Disease.

Mr Norman Capener, the senior surgeon (well, more than that, he really was the Princess Elizabeth, and the Princess Elizabeth was Mr Capener) was one of the foremost orthopaedic surgeons of his day, and just back from studying the latest methods in America when we arrived in North Devon. He was a short, dapper man, and whereas Mr Openshaw's hands had looked like a butcher's, his were of the plump pink starfish variety, so that one wondered, until one experienced their touch, how they ever had the strength, let alone the sensitivity, for the surgeon's trade.

The hospital which was Mr Capener's kingdom was new and small and run on a shoestring entirely for children. Two long wards, one for boys, one for girls, were separated in the middle by a glassed-in office. With what anxiety we watched the life going on in that fishbowl office, the comings and goings, Surgeon talking to Ward Sister, Sister giving orders to Staff Nurse, somebody writing up something on a chart. 'Is it something about me? I'm sure Sister looked this way. What are they going to do? Oh, please, God, don't let it be something *awful*!'

All down one side the wards were completely open on to a field; just a field, making no pretence of being a garden. It was lovely in fine summer weather, but murder in the winter, for staff and patients alike; worst of all in wild weather, when canvas screens had to be shipped all down the open side, blotting out the field and the sky along with the wind and the rain. But the rain spattered in over the top of the screens and the canvas bellied like the sails of a ship at sea, and the wind set the unshaded lights that hung on long flexes from the khaki-painted iron roof girders swinging wildly to and fro. Did I not say that the Princess Elizabeth was run on a shoestring?

There was a babies' ward, and there were a couple of side-wards where one recovered for forty-eight hours or so after an operation, or was quarantined for chickenpox; and where, occasionally, a child died. They never told us when that happened. They always said that the child had got better suddenly and gone home. But we always knew. Nothing ever happens in a children's hospital that is not instantly known.

There were long corridors behind the wards, with doors leading to operating theatre and X-ray room, plaster room and physio department and the domain of Mr Snow, the instrument maker. And presumably there were offices and nurses' quarters and kitchens and other such necessities of life elsewhere, but the two wards and their immediate surroundings, so far as we were concerned, made up the Princess Elizabeth Orthopaedic Hospital.

My memories of the times I spent there are confused, I think because they were so crowded. A hospital is a busy place at the best of times, the scene constantly in motion while remaining always the same, constant shift and change and hideous monotony swirling together like oil and water that mingle but never mix. I remember the staff better than my fellow patients because they did not change so often. Time and time I would go back to find the same doctors and nurses, whereas the child in the next bed would always be a stranger.

I remember Mr Capener of course, somewhat remote,

but always kindly and concerned. Mr Lillie, his second-in-command, a stocky, sandy-haired young man, who was not remote at all and if not in too desperate a hurry, was not above checking on his way through the ward to give some child who crossed his path (*me!* Oh, please let it be me!) a hug in passing. Matron was little and pretty, though quite old (I daresay she was forty) and wore a cap like a starched muslin columbine flower. Miss Tiller was the school mistress. Many of the children were long-term patients and school must go on. She came out of the same stable as Miss Axelin, though I do not think she had religious mania. She was just a plain uncomplicated bully in a brown overall, a woman without compassion or understanding, who could not believe that a child just out from the side-ward after an operation, still suffering the aftermath of anaesthetic and in more or less severe pain, was not capable of working quite a simple sum in long division, while a child waiting every moment to be summoned by the Physio for a probably painful session in the department — great reliance was put on forced movements in those days, and I have not forgotten the sickening experience of having a raw re-made joint forcibly opened and shut fifteen times or so — will not be able to concentrate his whole attention on the life of David Livingstone. We hated Miss Tiller; we would have poisoned her without compunction if the chance had come our way.

Then there was Sister Warde. We thought it shriekingly funny that a ward sister should be called Warde. She was a thoroughly nice kind girl, and we all liked her. For one thing, she was gentle. If she took your stitches out it didn't hurt nearly as much as if some other people did. But she had one failing, she had favourites; and unfortunately for me, I was one of them. That was partly the cause of the one time that I was ganged up on by my own kind. As with any shifting population, the whole tone of the ward would change from time to time; the children would be, on the whole, younger or older, gentler or rougher. During this particular sojourn of mine, the population of the girls' ward was older than usual, and a distinctly tough lot; and I was already in rather bad odour with them, because I came of a different background. I did not, I swear I did not, boast that my father was a naval officer, but when fathers were being discussed, I did not see the need to conceal the fact, since it was not shameful. I could not speak with the West Country tongue, I never have been able to; I wish I could, because it is a lovely tongue; and so I spoke differently from the rest. That was bad enough, but Sister Warde made things infinitely worse. And this was the way of it.

Food, in the Princess Elizabeth, was very plain and none too plentiful; so it was the custom for visiting parents to bring as much food as they liked, or could manage, and throughout visiting hours, which were only an hour and a half on Sundays and an hour every other Friday, we used to eat solidly, making up for the lean week gone by, and the lean week stretching ahead. It must have been an awe-inspiring sight, a long ward full of children all munching without pause, while their parents or aunties or friends plied them with more and yet more cake and bananas and chocolate. Not much time or energy left for communication — save that, as all baby sparrows know when they badger their mothers for food long after they are capable of feeding themselves, love can be communicated by the giving and receiving of food ... We were allowed to eat as much as we liked, or could, while visiting hour lasted, but when Staff had rung the bell for visitors to leave, and the tearful partings were over, a nurse would come round with a large tray, stopping at each bed with the question 'Anything to declare?' and anything that was over from the feast had to be handed in for the common good. Some of us tired of this, and took to hiding our loot under pillows and behind things in our lockers, and so the order went forth from Caesar that our beds were to be searched. I never hid anything. Maybe it was my horribly law-abiding upbringing, maybe it was just lack of initiative, maybe it was because when not actually hungry — and by the end of visiting hour I was about as hungry as a boa constrictor with a donkey inside it — I have never been very interested in sweet things; it certainly had nothing to do with virtue. But, alas, Sister Warde thought it had, and maybe hoping to shame the evil-doers, gave orders and gave them publicly, that my bed was to be exempt from the search. That put the lid on it. 'Sister's pet! Sister's pet!' chanted the rest of the ward; and I have never forgotten the sickening sense of shock with which I saw the face of an older girl, white and ugly with hostility between two black pigtails glowering at me as she delivered her accusation: '*You*'m the lady of the ward!'

And for the rest of that particular spell in hospital, I was an outcast, all shoulders turned in my direction. Nobody spoke to me except to get in a sly dig, nobody shared with me the small daily give and take of life. Luckily it was not very long before I went home; and the next time I came in there was a new population in the beds, and Sister Warde never made the same mistake again. But I have not forgotten what it feels like to be the stranger whom the pack turns on; nor that it was not a matter of whole children turning on a handicapped one, but of other handicapped children turning on one whose difference was that she spoke with a different accent from themselves.

But that was my only really bad memory of the Princess Elizabeth. There were many things which are not happy to remember. Operations: or not so much the operations themselves, as the night before, alone in the side-ward after one had been 'prepped' with razors and ether soup and given Bovril made with milk for supper because there would be no breakfast next morning, lying and staring at the green-shaded light, cut off from the world of the living which one could hear faintly going on in the ward outside; and the two days afterwards, muzzy and sick, and tied to a knee or elbow in a blood-soaked plaster, propped up with sandbags, sometimes in company with another child as wretched and homesick and in pain as oneself; and the mud-coloured walls, and the sterilizer in the corner casting odd shadows, and the sense of being imprisoned, almost entombed. And then there was the night I cried myself to sleep, actually cried, because next day was visiting day and I was so hungry that I did not think I would live to see it. One of the Up patients had eaten my supper. Supper was one piece of bread and butter per child, and the Up patients often helped bring it round, and they were hungry too. If one of them succumbed to temptation, somebody else went without. Somebody succumbed that evening, and my bed was the last in the ward. Then there was the constant dread of one's next session with the Physio; the time when chickenpox swept the hospital and there was no visiting for six weeks. The nagging weight of homesickness that went to sleep with me at night and was sitting on my chest waiting for me when I woke in the morning. The sense of utter powerlessness; no control over one's own destiny from whether one would or would not have an injection to whether one would or would not eat the egg custard which looked and tasted like sweetened scrambled eggs.

But there were the good things, too.

Generally speaking, we had fun together. We formed friendships as impermanent as the shipboard variety. There were treats and outings and entertainments, usually provided for us by Toc H or Rotary. I remember a concert party who came and performed for us on the grass in front of the wards, accompanied by the piano whose usual task was to play for school and the Sunday evening services. One very pretty girl in a pale blue Watteau shepherdess dress and a white cottonwool wig sang in a sweet little voice 'When Grandmama kissed Grandpapa in the second minuet'. But we preferred one of the local bank clerks in striped blazer and white flannel bags and a rakish boater, prancing up and down and singing, 'You've got me walking on the tips of my toes, And my hat's on the side of my head'.

There was the occasion which I remember with distinctly mixed emotions, when some of us went to the pantomime. I travelled with Matron in the back of an army ambulance stacked with six-foot boys on stretchers, and arrived feeling rather sick. All the boxes had been made over to us, and again I was fitted in behind a rampart of large boys lying on their fronts on stretchers. They behaved very badly throughout, and flipped screwed-up toffee papers onto the heads of the orchestra. I was convinced that everybody would think it was me! Oh, the shame of it! I sat rigid in the kind of agony that only a twelve-year-old knows in that kind of situation; and I remember nothing whatever of the performance. But in the interval there was one lovely, shimmering moment of pure magic, when the Fairy Queen, spangled as though straight off a Christmas tree, slipped in through the little dark doorway at the back of the box, and after her the Principal Girl and the Principal Boy, one at a time because there was no room for more, and the whole box seemed to light up with their presence, and the obnoxious boys paled into insignificance.

The second Guy Fawkes' party of my life took place during one of my spells in hospital. Toc H again. Most of the day they were at it, building a tall and imposing bonfire on the grass in front of the wards. At dusk our beds were all wheeled out, and we were muffled in extra blankets against the chill of the autumn evening and supplied with a constant flow of sparklers, which made a silvery firefly dance of light without any risk of setting oneself or the bedclothes on fire, while the experts got to work with the rockets (I no longer minded the bangs) and star shells and Catherine wheels.

But Mr Snow the instrument maker was really the star of the occasion. Some people believed that Mr Snow was, in West Country parlance 'not quite zackly'. But in truth I think he was just simple in the true sense of the word. He was short and plain and balding, with the gentlest of faces, and clear, quiet eyes. Ever after our first meeting, I pictured Tom Pinch of Dickens's *Martin Chuzzlewit* as looking exactly like Mr Snow. He loved children, and children loved him. He could not walk through the ward without being appealed to from all sides to 'Come and talk to me.' And however busy he was, he always came. He and his minions made all the splints and surgical appliances used in the hospital, and he would go to endless pains to make sure that there was no harsh edge left on a bi-valved plaster, and that the straps and kneecap of a calliper were shaped to give the maximum of comfort as well as doing their job. And to Mr Snow fell the job of making the Guy. It fell to him every year, but that particular November 5th was the only one I spent in hospital, and so I cannot speak for the rest. This Guy was superb: and the memory of him perched drunkenly on the crest of his splendid pyre has filled me with pitying scorn for almost every Guy I have seen since. He wore an old suit of Mr Capener's and a battered homburg hat, and had fireworks in his pockets and his ears and at his fingertips. Nothing very unusual about that. But his face and hands were skinned with a thin bright pink material used in those days for covering splints and keeping their padding in, so that he had a startling look of reality.

Skill and time and the love of the children who were to happily watch him burn had gone into his making. And all to be consumed in such a short time. But clearly it was all more than worthwhile to Mr Snow; and I remember the joy of the creative artist on his face, by the light of the sparkler he was holding like any other child, as his masterpiece — I am sure that that year's Guy must have been his masterpiece — found fulfilment in the flames.

Other junketings which helped to break the monotony of hospital routine happened more frequently. A local vicar held a short service on Wednesday evenings, and used to come round and talk to us afterwards; and a retired colonel with eyes like hot coals held a longer one on Sundays. His services somehow caught fire, and we looked forward to them surprisingly. But he never came round among us afterwards, which was sad. I think he might have done a lot of good if he had. And about once a week we had an aged Western or a Charlie Chaplin film after supper. For all these occasions, our beds used to be trundled into the boys' ward, or their beds into ours, and double parked. A certain amount of fraternisation was allowed at these times; but at all others we were expected to behave as though the other side did not exist. In fine weather the beds would live out on the concrete strip that divided the wards from the grass, and there was no barrier of glassed-in office between the first bed of the girls' ward and the last bed of the boys'. But any attempt to signal across the gulf was a heinous crime. Sometimes the boys tried to smuggle notes, and that was bad enough; but if a girl tried it, that was the ultimate in depravity. Boys were nasty, and girls who wanted to have anything to do with boys were horrid. Occasionally those of us who were up would pass boys in the corridor on the way to the physio department or the X-ray room; but when that happened, we must pass without speaking or even looking.

If we were 'In' long enough, we actually got indoctrinated with all this, and took a pride in considering the boys' ward a kind of enemy territory. What the Powers That Be thought we were going to do to each other I can't imagine; corridors were long and straight, devoid of cover and scarcely ever empty of nurses. And most of us, on both sides of the gulf, were encased in plaster from chest to heel, or attached to our own bed by frameworks and weights and pulleys like something out of a mediaeval torture chamber. Added to which, the majority of us were under twelve, which really was quite young in those days.

For the weekly Guide meetings, the beds of the Hospital Company were pushed together in one corner of the ward and we wore dark blue hats and yellow ties even when the rest of us was too deep in plaster to wear anything at all. I had long wanted to be a Girl Guide, and here was my chance. I was proud and happy as I struggled to learn my knots — to this day, I can only tie a reef knot by first tying a grannie, and then noticing what I have done wrong. I learned tracking signs and Morse Code. Pride swelled in my breast, when, my Tenderfoot weeks behind me, I took my Guide Promise, and became a fully-fledged third-class Guide. At home, I was transferred to a Post Guide Company. But guiding on one's own, with only a monthly magazine and occasional visits from one's Guider leaves much to be desired. The Hospital Company, in which I belonged to the Traveller's Joy Patrol, was something very much on the credit side of being in hospital. I was a bad Guide; I never rose above second class, and never won any badges but my Artist's Badge. But I did win the Guides' equivalent to the Scouts' Jack Cornwell Medal.

I have seriously wondered whether I should set that down in this account of my young days. Does it come under the heading of boasting, the next most shameful thing to crying in public? But it is true, and it is part of me, and I have set down things of which I am ashamed. My mother had brought me up to be as near as possible a cross between a Red Indian brave and that annoying Spartan youth with a fox under his cloak. That was not very near, to be sure, but perhaps I was slightly above average in the gentle art of bearing pain. I was certainly better at it then than I am now. And I suppose that as a result I got through a string of operations with marginally less than average fuss. Well, I must have done, because suddenly I found myself being awarded the Fortitude Badge. I have it still, pushed away as far as possible in the back of a drawer, because the actual badge really is rather shame-making; a purple enamel cross with the Guide badge in the middle, hanging on a purple ribbon from a purple enamel bar, with 'Fortitude' blazoned on it in gold. Why we girls should have this monstrosity foisted on us while boys receive the perfectly respectable Jack Cornwell medal, I do not know. It is enough to turn one to Women's Lib.

But nothing of that bothered me at the time. I was basking in a kind of small boy's hour of glory, anyway; full of the warm knowledge that my father and mother were proud of me. Truth to tell, I was rather proud of myself.

The great day came. All the Company's beds were pushed together. I was Up, at that time, and therefore able to appear in full uniform. Oh, the pride with which I wore the hideous blue cotton tunic, yellow tie and squashy blue hat! My father and mother came, Mr Capener came, Matron came, Lady Clinton, the County Commissioner, came to do the presentation. I was well drilled beforehand by our Captain, who was also the hospital secretary. When she called me out, I was to advance, and take my stand in front of Lady Clinton, who would pin on the badge and shake hands with me and then speak a few words to me and to the

Company in general. And when she had finished speaking to me personally, I was to march back to my place and stand smartly until she had finished altogether. I was doubtful as to how I should know the exact moment for retreat, but Captain said she would waggle her eyebrows at me when the moment came. So there was Lady Clinton, and there was I, swollen with pride, while she pinned the thing onto my meagre chest; and so far, all going beautifully. But either the strain of having the County Commissioner in our midst was too much for Captain, and she forgot to give the signal, or I failed to pick it up. And so there I remained, standing to attention under Lady Clinton's bust (I was small for my age) and gazing up past it into her face, and wondering why she was gradually going that kind of dusky shade of pink and apparently forgetting her lines.

Years later I learned that in guiding circles I had the reputation of being the only person who had ever put Lady Clinton out of countenance.

But my most vivid and enduring memory of the Princess Elizabeth concerns a book. The rigid segregation of the sexes applied even to our reading matter. We did not have a hospital library; we had two ward libraries, ours housed in a cupboard, the boys' piled on a large table in the corridor just outside their ward door. When I was Up, and going to the physio department under my own steam, I used to pass it on my daily journeys to and fro; and how I envied the boys their library! There was of course no money to buy books; we depended entirely upon the kind hearts of the general public, who unloaded onto us the unwanted books they found in their attics during spring-cleaning. So, to start with, our books were those which somebody else didn't want; and as soon as they reached the hospital they were rigidly divided up; Boys' Library, Girls' Library, with anything that remotely resembled an adventure story going to the Boys'. Unfortunately most of the books with any quality about them seemed to fall under this heading. Passing the Boys' Library I used to eye with longing battered copies of *Treasure Island*, *King Solomon's Mines* or *Tom Brown's Schooldays*. Our own library cupboard seemed to be entirely stocked with Victorian stories about little girls of great virtue who died young, generally of consumption, surrounded by grieving friends; or the American version of the same theme, which was even worse. There was one about a little girl whose brutal father beat her for preaching total abstinence to the clientele of his public house. She died of consumption, too. It wasn't really much of an incentive to virtue. There were a few books by Mrs Ewing and Louisa M Alcott, but they were very definitely the aristocracy of our bookshelves; and myself, I have never been an Alcott fan.

And then one day I found a book.

It was a book called *Emily of New Moon*, about a little girl whose father died of consumption — that made a change, to start with — after which she was brought up by strict aunts in an old farmhouse somewhere in Canada. A Canadian story, not an American one; but I barely registered that at the time. What made it so different from other books of its kind I did not know, and I do not really know even now. But for me it was magic. I carried it off and kept it under my pillow or clutched to my bosom at bed-making time, and it seems as though I read it all that summer long, which can scarcely have been the fact; but I think I must have read it through, at first voraciously and then with slow and lingering delight, at least three times on the trot. And it was summer. On fine summer nights the beds remained out on the concrete strip all night, and I used to read, half under the bedclothes to evade Night Nurse's eagle eye, until the last dregs of the light had drained away, and the first stars pricked out in a sky of witchball green; and from the barracks half a mile away, the bugles sounding Last Post had a magic in them, too, that turned them into the horns of Elfland, faintly blowing.

The Evening Star, and the bugles sounding across the misty fields in the summer dusk, and the book hidden under the bed-clothes somehow entered into each other and became part of the same enchantment, while I followed spellbound Emily's adventures and misadventures, her fantasies and her budding relationships, and her first attempts to be a writer. Was that the secret of the book's attraction? No, I do not think so, my own first quickening in that direction was still around eight years away. It was just magic, and magic is always an unaccountable thing.

The time came to go home, and *Emily of New Moon* was left behind me. I never forgot the book, and by fits and starts in later years I tried to trace it. But by then, of course, it was too late. I did not even know who it was by; and gradually I let it go. Maybe it was better that way. Once I even read *Anne of Green Gables*, but did not recognise the hand, though the family likeness seems clear enough to me now.

And then, only a few years ago, a Canadian friend and fellow writer mentioned in a letter that she was doing a 'piece' for a children's literature magazine on the works of L M Montgomery, and had been remaking the acquaintance of *Anne of Green Gables*, and all the author's other Annes and Kates and Emilys. And suddenly the penny dropped, or perhaps, writing of such an author, I should say that somewhere a little silver bell rang loud and clear.

By return of post, I wrote off to my friend, 'Please, please, is the Emily you mention by any chance *Emily of New Moon*?' and told her the whole story, as I have told it here. Back came her reply. It was, it is! It was still in print in paperback, and she would send me a copy! A few weeks later it arrived; and no mere modern paperback. Bless the girl, she had found me the real thing; a secondhand hardbacked copy, well worn, and with a pale ring on the faded cover, where some previous owner had set down her mug of hot milk on it!

And now that I had it, I was almost afraid to open it and begin reading. It was a little like going back to a place where one was happy, years ago, even meeting an old love, Would the specialness, the magic, still be there? I know someone who has never been able to read *The Cuckoo Clock* since leaving her girlhood home, because it had to be read sitting halfway up the stairs, where the light through a stained-glass landing window fell on it, staining the pages red and blue and green. How if it was like that with Emily?

I took the book to bed with me that night, opened it and started reading. And the magic was still there! Even without the evening star and the distant bugle, it was still there! But in a strange way it was not without them, for they had entered into *Emily of New Moon* and were still there, waiting for me; a small fragment of my own childhood given back to me again.

And so now Emily, complete with milky mug-stain, lives on the broad windowsill of my bedroom, along with *The Wind in the Willows* and *The Tailor of Gloucester*, *The Lady's Not for Burning*, Brian Hooker's translation of *Cyrano de Bergerac* and a few more of my nearest and dearest books. And I still do not really know why it has the right to be there.

13

I left school at fourteen, which you could do in those days. It was painfully obvious that it was not going to be the least use my staying on any longer. The only subject I was any good at was art — I had been good at that since I was five and began decorating my plasters with rather magnificent robins in brown and red chalk. So I left St George's and went to Bideford Art School, which really was an art school, and an extremely good one at that time. It was more of a technical college when I last heard of it.

Three mornings a week my mother drove me in by the 'short' road, made up of wandering lanes between high banks. The banks were starred in springtime with primroses and celandines and the little wild daffodils known in the West Country as Lent Lilies; purple-pink with foxglove spires and overhung with elder in summer, when the cow parsley brushed the car on both sides as one drove by. It was six miles, and my mother, who always claimed to be a nervous driver, did the trip, door to door, in ten minutes. Some people became not merely nervous, but nervous wrecks, after driving with her, but I got acclimatised — though I don't think the car ever did, for she drove rather as though she was riding a horse with spurs and a wolf-bit, in a series of wild jerks and crashing gears. But we always got there in the end, and there at the art school I would be left with my painting gear and a packet of sandwiches, to be picked up again at the end of the afternoon session.

I used to slightly, very slightly, dread the sandwich lunch hour, when everybody else had gone off, and I was alone in the long bare empty rooms with the high windows; sharing the emptiness with the cold white casts of the Apollo Belvedere, and Cylene's weary horse from the Parthenon, and Fred the skeleton in his green cupboard on casters. Still, it did not last long, for generally Mortimer Gould would hurry through his own break and come back early to see that I was all right. Gould was eighteen and played the violin in a dance orchestra in the evenings to help pay his way.

Everybody was eighteen or more, except me. At fourteen, I was very much the baby of the art school; the others were all nice to me, Gould the nicest of all, but of course they didn't include me in anything. So art school for me really was all work and no play. Not that I am complaining; I loved the work, and I stuck to it harder than I had ever stuck to anything before. I did a full three-year stint, taking the General Art Course. The white plaster casts of classical statuary I made studies of, from the North, South, East and West, in pencil, charcoal, oils and water colours. I did Still Life, Portraiture, Composition and Design. I did Life — occasionally we had a paid girl model for that, but more often it was a young fisherman from the Quay, posing bashfully in a G-string for 7/6d an hour. Once it was a hard-up divinity student who, for some unknown reason, having taken off everything else, refused to take off his shoes, socks or sock-suspenders.

In due course, I passed my City & Guilds exams and until quite recently, when I looked for them and they were nowhere to be found, used to boast that I had my diplomas to prove it. I came out top of all Britain for an oil still-life done in precisely two and a half hours with an adjudicator breathing down my neck, of an oilcan, bar of soap, scrubbing-brush, one of those string dishcloths draped in the background, and an orange. My ambition soared; my earliest and most cherished ambition was to be the first woman President of the Royal Academy!

Always, behind the changes of school — hospital — art school, was the continuity of home, our own particular hilltop two and a half miles from nowhere. My own bedroom with one window looking out into the lilac tree, and Orion swinging in at the other; and the birds and animals that shared the hilltop with us. So far into the wild, and with the wood so close around us, we had such a richness of birds; not only the thrushes and blackbirds and robins and bluetits that gardens know. We had all those, of course, but goldcrests and treecreepers as well, grey wagtails and willow-warblers and nuthatches, and yellowhammers flittering like blown sunshine along the garden hedge, and the curlews at mating time, and the buzzards mewing as they swung their sky-wide circles above the fields. Rabbits ate everything in the garden, and red squirrels lived in the wood, foxes barked through our winter nights, while owls perched on the chimney to warm their feet, and made eerie noises down to us in the sitting-room below. And one hard winter, through the kitchen window, we saw an ermine, a stoat in his full winter white, frisking along the bank between the garden and the wood.

I knew and loved the country immediately round us with a bond of intimacy that has not held me to any countryside since. I had graduated from my spinal carriage entirely soon after we came to live in North Devon. I could, in fact, walk reasonably well; and my mother was determined that I should be able to walk two miles. If you could walk two miles, she said, you could get to most places you needed to get to. Actually, this is a fallacy. The fact that you can, with great difficulty, and taking an unconscionable time about it, walk two miles, will not get you anywhere you need, or at any rate want, to go. There were times when a wheelchair would have added another dimension to my life, but that was a forbidden subject; and it was not until many, many years later, long after my father and I were alone, that I took the law into my own hands and bought one; and instantly, dazzled with the new freedom that it brought me, swept my father off to his old haunts on an Hellenic cruise.

So, in training for this two miles, on art-school-free afternoons, my mother and I went for walks.

From our drive gate, which marked the joining place of three parishes and had once been the site of the local gallows, one road led towards Yarnscombe, one towards Barnstaple, and the third towards Huntshaw Cross half a mile away, where you could choose again, turning right, the 'short' road to Bideford, or left towards Huntshaw, or keeping straight on towards Torrington by a road giving a wonderful view over Bideford Bay to Lundy floating on the skyline. And all these roads we walked in rotation, my mother and Mike the Airedale, and me, while my father worked in the garden or wrote more Sailing Directions for the Admiralty.

My feelings about those walks were somewhat mixed. Both physically and emotionally they could be something of an ordeal; for sometimes I was just not in good walking trim, and if my performance was worse than average, this upset my mother, who would fight back by telling me yet again how much she had sacrificed for me, sometimes even adding that she had known how it would be before I was born and had never wanted to have me at all. But there were other days when nothing went wrong, and we would poke about the hedges for the first celandines and laugh at silly jokes, and my mother would sing songs as we went along that had been taught her in her childhood by the cook. And we would meet and have most interesting conversations with Mr Rodd the local poacher, who was always looking for a strayed bullock, and had been looking for it for thirty years, with a twelve-bore under his arm; or with our favourite roadman, who had had most of his face blown off in the war and was a mine of information about birds' nests and vipers and weather and all kinds of country lore.

In the course of those walks I came to know one small patch of country at every time of the year, in all weathers and all moods, and but for them, I think I would have less skill in writing of country things than I have now. Once I even kept a kind of nature diary for the round of a whole year, recording the first honeysuckle leaves like tiny green praying hands in the January hedges, the first cuckoo, a blue haze over the summer hills, a squall of rain, the scent of the little creamy Man Orchis in a damp ditch, the sowing and harvesting of winter wheat. I had it for years. But like so many other things, it got lost when my father and I left North Devon.

As the years went by I began to be more and more conscious of being lonely. It had not really mattered until I was fourteen, the isolation in which we lived. There was school, and there was hospital. I was never allowed to bring anyone home from school, I am still not sure why, but I think my mother feared other links as a menace, and so I never made any real friends there, aware, I think, of the uselessness of trying to do so. And hospital was a world of its own. When one left, the door shut behind one until the next time, and any tentative friendships were left behind. But until I was fourteen, school and hospital did provide points of contact with my own generation. Art school was another matter; it was Sheerness Dockyard all over again, for between fourteen and eighteen-to-twenty lies a generation gap almost as great as between fourteen and five. And at the same time as I left school, I became too old for a children's hospital. From then on, when I fell due for another operation, I retired into a nursing-home in Exeter, and a nursing-home can be one of the loneliest places in the world. Admittedly, this one had a large walled garden with a mulberry tree, and convalescent patients could be moved out into little shelters like rabbit-hutches in it. But as any Up patients who dropped in on me were usually dotty old ladies under the impression that I was their younger sister who had been dead for fifty years, or bent on telling me a long story about the Archdeacon coming to call on a Thursday — or was it a Tuesday? — not long after they got married, I gained little real companionship from their visits.

I was beginning to need companionship sorely. I was fifteen, sixteen, seventeen, and didn't know a soul of my own age. Living so far in the country was not really ideal for a young thing with mobility problems. My father and mother had each other, and though we were a very close-knit family, in any triangular group of father, mother and child, in the very nature of things, however much the parents make him their companion, the child is going to be odd man out, and therefore needs other contacts. I do not think my father saw this, and I am very sure my mother did not.

Once, a visiting aunt saw, and had a word with my mother about it, but my mother was so sure she was mistaken that she was not even really upset; only she told me about it afterwards, adding, 'We don't need anybody but each other, do we?' And I, I had not the ruthlessness, or perhaps the courage, to say to her, 'Yes, I do. I love you, and we are as close as ever a mother and daughter were to each other. But I need friends of my own age. I need to be a person in my own right.'

My mother, much as she had loved parties in her young days, no longer seemed to want any social life, and my father had contacts of another kind; he went shooting with a group of old friends every week through the winter, and sat on the Parish Council and things of that sort; and for the rest, if he could have my mother, and Mike and me tagging along immediately behind, I think he wanted nothing more.

They were a crazily assorted couple; my father so quiet and steady and unimaginative, so simple in his approach to things, in some ways so much the product of his Puritan and Quaker forebears; my mother so mercurial, living half the time in a fantasy world of her own devising. Part of her trouble, I think, was that she had a *prima donna* temperament without a *prima donna* outlet. If she could have been a great tragic actress, a Mrs Patrick Campbell, she might have got it all out of her system on the stage and been quite normal about the house. As it was, she played out her roles in her everyday life. She would get up in the morning as Polly Linton, the Madcap of the IVth. Halfway through breakfast something would happen — maybe my father or I would say or do something, or not say or do something; in either case we seldom discovered what, or maybe some change of mood would take place of its own accord within her — and we would find that we were eating toast and marmalade in company with Lady Macbeth; and Lady Macbeth would be with us for the rest of the day, or three days, or a fortnight. And then, as suddenly as she had come, Lady Macbeth would depart, and in her place, joy of joys, would be the Rose of Tralee. My mother had no drop of Irish blood in her, but had spent long summer holidays with Irish relatives when she was a child, and when she had been absolutely horrible for days (and if ever a woman knew how to be horrible, she did, putting the boot in to all our sensitive spots with a sure instinct for where it would hurt most), and was suddenly nice again, indeed whenever she had the urge to be particularly charming, she would become Irish of the Irish. My father used to just wait patiently for the black mood to depart; I was less patient, and went in for silent inward rebellion. I used to say to myself, 'This time she's done it once too often! This time I won't come running the instant she smiles at me. *Two can play at that game!*' But always, when the sun did come out again, I was so relieved and so overjoyed to be forgiven, along with my father, for our unknown crime that I would come running as before.

It became accepted that my mother had depressions; but in those days all that happened when you had depressions was that the doctor gave you a tonic or a weak bromide mixture and a pep-talk, and even your nearest and dearest couldn't help feeling that if only you would pull yourself *together* ... I believe she really was what we should now call manic depressive, and probably needed some kind of treatment. And maybe the sorrows and anxieties that I had caused her had a lot to do with it; but I do also truly believe that a large part of her trouble stemmed from this problem of having an outsize artistic temperament and no safety-valve. I, who had any tendencies to a temperament of any kind firmly extinguished when very young, and have the safety-valve of creative writing — except when suffering from Writer's Block — should count my blessings, and be thankful to my mother for something of her mind and imagination that I have inherited from her,

So, there we were, a triangle with my parents in their odd way linked and complementary to each other across the top; my mother reaching down from her corner to keep a tight hold on me at all times, and on the third side, the side that joined my father and me, a very much more normal father-and-daughter relationship, which had none of the intensity or the sense of captivity on my part which bedevilled the link between my mother and myself. But still, the solitary point at the bottom of the triangle, there was I.

And I was horribly and increasingly lonely.

14

When I was seventeen, I fell in love with my cousin Edward. At least, I thought I did.

It was the last summer before the war, and he came to spend part of his leave with us. I had seen him very occasionally since the Sheerness days, but those few occasions have left no particular mark on my memory. And now suddenly, there he was, a lieutenant in the Navy, and with war beginning to loom, which made him seem a prospective hero. I was young for my age, and had not yet grown out of hero-worship. He was almost the first young man I had ever spoken to; and certainly he was the first who ever appeared to notice that I was a girl. He opened doors for me and got up when I came into the room, and looked at me intently and as though my opinions mattered when we talked to each other. And I was his slave, just as surely as I was at five years old when he noticed that I was human and brought me unlawful coconut from Sheerness Fair.

All that summer is coloured in my memory by two things: by the growing shadow of war despite Mr Chamberlain's assurance that it was 'peace in our time', and by the fact that I was in love with Edward. Later, much later, I found that it was only what people who are too old to experience it themselves call calf-love, after all. But I could not know that at the time, and calf-love is as sweet and as bitter as the real thing, when one does not know what the real thing is. It is real, too, only different, belonging to an earlier season in life; and I have always been glad that I did not have to finish my growing up without it. I knew of course that it was not returned, but for the present it was enough just to be in love, to experience the sudden added butterfly sheen to life, to dream a few dreams and weave a few romantic fantasies, and even — for I was after all my mother's daughter — to be a Tragic Figure. My mother knew what had happened, and was sympathetic, which is surprising when one comes to think of it; my father, bless him, remained in complete ignorance. Edward himself, I don't know; I expect he guessed.

We went for picnics and for days out in the car, as we always did in time of summer visitors. And as we had my Uncle Cyril and his wife with us at the same time — she was the aunt who had had the abortive few words with my mother on my account, the previous year — we had to take two cars. I generally managed to go in Edward's, sitting beside him in the front seat, since one of the few advantages of stiffened knees is that they make the back seats of cars virtually impossible. And I remember watching his hands on the wheel and gear lever, and noticing how like they were to my father's, only longer fingered and darker skinned. He was a very dark young man altogether, black-haired, olive-skinned, with eyes of a hot red-brown. Nothing else of him was like my father at all, except that they both had broken noses. In Edward's case this had endowed him with a peculiar one-sided sniff, which he used for purposes of derision, superior to anything of the sort that I have heard before or since.

Once in Edward's car, I would do my best to forget that there were other people in the back seat. And we would head for Clovelly or Lynmouth, or the nearer fringes of Dartmoor, all subtly different from their old selves, instinct with a new significance, glowing in softer and more brilliant colours, because I was in love with Edward, and because everything might be coming to an end, anyway, with a war darkening on the skyline — though Edward said no, and Edward could surely not be mistaken.

The end of Edward's leave came, and he went back to his

ship. I wore a tiny photo of him cut out of a snapshot in a silver locket round my neck and never took it off day or night, and another year went by. I was eighteen, and on that beautiful September Sunday in 1939 the war came.

Two days before the official declaration, my father went off to his first command, the *Mooltan*, an armed merchant cruiser. And my mother and I were on our own, with Belgie from the village — all our maids came from the village, mostly from the same family — and of course with Mike to guard us and the house. Mike was eight years old by that time, a grand chap, who combined being a magnificent house dog with a tender-hearted love for all young things, whether human children, calves or ducklings, that would have been more at home in a labrador bitch. He was very much a one-man dog, the one man being my father, and we wondered somewhat anxiously, among all the other anxieties of the time, how he would settle down without him. But it seemed that Mike was a philosopher. With my father gone, he gave first place in his life to my mother, though always returning to his old allegiance when my father came home on leave. His relationship with me remained what it always had been, an easy and undemanding friendship between equals.

We settled down into the wartime routine that was to last for six years. Living in the depth of the country, so far from any target area, in some ways we never saw the war at all. We had only three jettisoned bombs within a mile of us from first to last; and my mother and I both had a regretful feeling that we were missing out on something that the rest of the country was sharing, though there must have been many in the same case as ourselves. That is not to say that they were easy years for either of us. We had our full share of the anxieties of women with their menfolk away at the wars. The armed merchant cruisers — converted passenger ships with antiquated guns — whose chief duty if the convoy in their charge was attacked was to engage the enemy against completely hopeless odds, and be blown out of the water while their charges got away, soon gained themselves the name of 'The Suicide Squad'. My father lost a good many old friends in that way, including Captain Kennedy of the *Rawalpindi*. So it was not much wonder that my mother's depressions grew worse than ever, and she took to threatening suicide from time to time. Since she never inflicted her dark times on any but her most beloved, Belgie escaped entirely, and I was left to bear the full brunt of them alone, and cope with them as best I could single-handed. For whereas at fourteen, you tend to merely grit your teeth and wait for it to go away, at eighteen plus you feel that you have to do something, try to help in some way. Not that it was ever the least use. My mother wearing her Lady Macbeth hat was beyond the reach of help or reason, and the more she needed it the more I could not reach her.

There were the times between the black patches, of course. And a wartime routine of a kind that I think quite a lot of people beside myself remember affectionately. Long, lamp-lit evenings when the black-out curtains were drawn, for Calor gas was soon unobtainable and we were back to the soft light of lamps, and the lamp-smitch smell of La Delicia. We went to bed by candlelight, too. The anxious listening to the news three times a day, the struggles with ration books and the old man who did the heavy gardening, and under whose hand nothing thrived that he did not plant himself, which would not have mattered if he had ever planted anything but white alyssum and leeks. *ITMA* and *Happidrome* on the wireless, and *Children's Hour*. What marvellous *Children's Hours* we had in the war! And my mother reading aloud to both of us in the afternoons, while I worked. Mercifully she had at long last accepted that I was never really going to be able to walk two miles at a stretch, and our afternoon treks had slackened off. There being, apparently, no other war work that I could do, I had managed to get myself on to the team of a dictatorial old lady who collected handicraft materials and sent them out to prisoner of war camps and camp hospitals in Germany, and I was generally working out tapestry designs and painting them on to canvas for her. It was funny sort of war work, but better than nothing,

For the first part of the war, we were the Signals Post for the local company of the Home Guard, captained by one Mr MacDonald, who in civilian life was Lord Clinton's forester. We were the only phone for miles, besides having the big Stoep and the outbuildings, and so were the obvious choice. They became a part of our life. On winter nights of wind and rain the lulls in the storm were filled with their cheerful laughter at 3 am; for though Mr MacDonald had issued strict orders that the men on duty with us were to take their boots off so as not to disturb us, nothing could be done, of course, about their sense of humour and happy appreciation of each other's dirty stories. On fine summer days they sat in deckchairs on the lawn, while my mother or I took their phone calls for them. Their despatch rider was a somewhat gormless youth with a motor-bike and a cleft palate, so they used him as seldom as possible, preferring to rely on us and the telephone.

Wonderful stories we used to hear, of exercises and manoeuvres; the ironmonger-corporal describing how he had come, the previous night, to 'kill' two Germans and an umpire. The 'Germans' had taken him by surprise when he was hurrying somewhere on his push-bike, and a nearby umpire had upheld their claim to have put him out of action. But our valiant ironmonger, unarmed but not to be so easily daunted when the fate of the civilised world was at stake, had got up, pointed two fingers at them and said, 'Bang, bang, bang! You're all dead.' And got back on his bicycle and rode off, while they were still arguing.

After the first year or so, when things got better organised and more professional and our company of Dad's Army departed elsewhere, we were sorry to see them go, though certainly the nights were quieter and the tea ration went further without them.

We had a supplementary allowance of petrol, because, as my mother wrote on the application form that had to go in every three months, her daughter was crippled and could not use public transport. How my stomach cringed every time we arrived at that bit — and come to think of it, there *was* no public transport, and never had been, in that neck of the woods, except for the market bus to Barnstaple on Fridays. At all events, we had our extra petrol ration, and so we were able to manage a weekly shopping day. On Thursdays we went in to Torrington and did the first half of the shopping: grocer, ironmonger, garage, post office, bank, a three- and-sixpenny lunch in the café in the Square. Then we went on into Bideford to do the afternoon shopping: fishmonger, butcher for our microscopic portions of meat and spam and whatever in the way of lights and the more unsavoury scraps of offal could be scraped together for Mike. There was Mr Harper's lovely bookshop where we changed library books, and where I read in hurried and indigestible gulps many a book that I could not afford to buy, including the whole seven volumes of Frazer's *Golden Bough*, coming back week after week to take my treasure into a secluded corner and read and read while my mother went off about other things.

Mr Harper looked like everyone's idea of an Oxford professor, and his own branch of the business was the antiquarian section. One day I found him sitting in the middle of his labyrinth of dusty volumes like a disconsolate minotaur because he had accidentally sold a copy of Gerard's *Herbal*, and sold it to an American at that so that it was lost, not only to him, but to England.

But I could not frequent Sidney Harper's Sons every week. Sometimes I would have a painting job on hand, and my mother would drop me off at the Art School, while she did the shopping on her own. I was no longer a student, having finished my General Art Course the year before the war, but by courtesy of Mr Sharpe, my old headmaster, I was allowed the use of an empty room whenever I had a sitter. For by now I was a professional miniature painter.

How grand, and how ladylike and old-fashioned that sounds! It was not entirely by my own choice. I had loved working in oils; but when I finished as a student, everybody, my mother and father, Mr Sharpe, all advised me to become a miniature painter. They pointed out that I would never be able to handle a big canvas; and I did not at that time know that the *Mona Lisa* is only something like seventy-seven by fifty-three centimetres, and so had no argument to use against them. So I took a crash course with an old man in Paignton who was both a first-class miniaturist himself and a superb teacher, and became, still with a lingering lack of enthusiasm — apart from anything else, I was sure that no miniaturist was likely to become the first woman President of the Royal Academy — a miniature painter myself.

I was quite a good one. Technically I was a very good one; but technique is not everything. I began to get sitters; and since the petrol situation made it impossible for people to get out to us, and Bideford was a good central point, I had this arrangement with Mr Sharpe. I painted children for the most part. Oh, the awfulness of trying to paint children, who can never sit still for a second, even when being told stories; and even more, the awfulness of their mothers, who are never satisfied, and who equate blue eyes and duckling yellow hair with beauty! But as the war went on, I began to get more and more work to do at home from photographs; husbands and sons in the uniform of one or other of the services. And then, sadly, more and more often, photographs of husbands and sons who would not be coming home again.

I have said before that my mother claimed to have 'the Sight', and that her flashes of foreknowing did come true just often enough to make them uncomfortable — for she generally foresaw disaster. I have inherited only a kind of residual trace of 'the Sight' from her, and, at least so far, have only had about three or four flashes of foreknowledge in my life. But one of them came to me in the first spring of the war. It was quite small and not involving any disaster, but not to be denied. My father's photograph and Edward's stood side by side on a broad windowsill in the sitting-room. And one day, glancing at them in passing as I crossed the room, I knew with absolute certainty that I should be seeing both of them again before many days were out.

There was no immediate prospect of my father getting leave; and Edward, so far as I knew, was in the Pacific. But I did not even try telling myself not to be silly, that I was indulging in wishful thinking. I simply knew. All that remained was to wait until it happened.

Sure enough, within a week, the *Mooltan* had come into Devonport for a refit and to have more antiquated guns added to her armament. Mike had been parked with Belgie and her family, and my mother and I were buzzing down to Devonport on long-hoarded petrol.

We spent a fortnight in a Plymouth hotel, and went on board nearly every day. I loved being half of the Captain's womenfolk, spoiled and cosseted by Grindley, my father's steward, who produced hot buttered toast for tea even under the most unlikely conditions such as when the entire galley was out of action. The *Mooltan* was a dear old ship, nearly as broad as she was long. The steadiest seaboat he'd ever met, my father said. Also, alas, the slowest. All ships have their own atmosphere, and hers was strong and kindly, like an old good-humoured cart mare. And my father was so happy with her.

The days went by, and there was no sign of Edward, and I began to get anxious in an odd sort of way, not because I doubted that he would come, I knew he would, but the time was getting so short and I didn't see how. And then almost on the last day my father received a signal that he was in Devonport in transit from one ship to another and had just learned that the *Mooltan* was there too ...

So we had a tea party on board, with more of Grindley's hot buttered toast, and I had a few minutes alone with Edward in the Captain's day cabin while my father and mother went off somewhere on their own. A few minutes to last me the whole war; and so far as I remember we never spoke one word that the whole ship could not have listened to without interest. But I was happy. Looking back, I think that I was happy with rather pathetically little.

There was a lot happening in Plymouth, as everywhere else that May, a lot of sorrow and desperate anxiety and hope and heartbreak. For it was Dunkirk time. I think I shall never forget the sight of the lorries and ambulances and buses bringing men up from the docks. Many were wounded. Some, in a kind of drunkenness of breaking strain, waving their arms and blowing kisses to every woman they passed. Some, sitting like zombies, the husks of men, blind and leaden with exhaustion.

Among our fellow guests in the hotel were three women waiting for husbands. One got back draped in a blanket, having lost his trousers on the beaches; one had not arrived by the time we left ...

That spring also I had my first miniature in the Royal Academy. Not a portrait, but a 'subject miniature' — head and shoulders of a knight in fifteenth-century armour, a banner with St George's cross flying behind him. It was called 'Spirit of England' and was highly romanticised. I was a very romantic girl, and it showed badly in my paintings, as Edward never scrupled to point out. But it caught the mood of the moment and sold on the first day and got itself written up in various papers. The news went round the hotel like wildfire and I was showered with congratulations until my head was in danger of bursting. My father was unashamedly a dog with ten tails and all of them wagging; but when anybody said to my mother that she must be proud of me, she smiled deprecatingly down her beautifully shaped nose. 'Oh, why? God gave her her gift. All she has done is to make proper use of it.' Only in private to me she said, 'Duckie, I *do* so enjoy being humble!'

Sometimes, in trying to write about my mother, I feel as though I was writing about two different people; or three — or four.

15

Our war — my mother's and mine — went on as before. Past the Battle of Britain and the North African campaign and the doodle-bugs. My father came and went. About a year after Dunkirk the *Mooltan* was attacked by German dive-bombers in the Western Approaches and badly mauled, though she was lucky and survived. And my father, privately asked for his opinion, had no choice but to tell Their Lordships of the Admiralty that as an armed merchant cruiser she was an even better death-trap than most.

So after a complete refit and vast repairs, she became a troop transport, and my father, much to his disgust, was sent up to Liverpool, to take charge of the Western Approach repair yards.

From the very first, he campaigned to get out of it all and back to sea. But he was making too good a job of things where he was; and it was two years before he got to sea again, this time as a Commodore of Convoys. In that job he was supremely happy, though it did not provide him with the command of his own ship. His command, in fact, was the convoy. He would board his appointed ship — generally a Norwegian, for the Norwegian cargo vessels had accommodation for eight or ten passengers, just right for one Commodore and his staff — and take the convoy to its appointed destination; wait there for the return convoy, and repeat the process. He got on splendidly with the Norwegian skippers, who, one after another, taught or tried to teach him to play chess. And since he never drank anything stronger than cocoa at sea — Sir Christopher Cradock had told him, twenty-five years before, 'If you run your ship on the beach, and you've had half a pint of beer in the past twenty-four hours, they'll break you. Never have a drink from the moment you leave harbour, and at least you're safe from that charge' — he always found a couple of bottles of something in his cabin when the trip was over, to make up for what he had not drunk on board. Usually it was schnapps, but once it was Drambuie and by the end of the war he had quite a nice little cellar, which came in useful on special occasions for years afterwards.

We always took a warm interest in where he was going, not that we ever knew until he was back again, and not just the interest of anxious and loving womenfolk — a far more mercenary interest than that; because according to where he went, were the things he brought home. Oranges and Turkish delight — sweet and sticky Turkish delight in those sugar-starved days! — when the convoy was to and from Gibraltar; nylons from Bloomingdales in Fifth Avenue, New York, when it was America. I am afraid our first question on receiving him back each time was, 'What have you brought us?' The only time we got nothing was when he took the very last Russian convoy of the war. All he brought back that time was a great deal of bitterness. The authorities had informed him that he might go ashore if he wished, but that the permission did not extend to his men. Naturally he had not gone ashore. But he had seen, piled and rotting on the docksides, war supplies which earlier convoys, in the days when the Russian run was synonymous with a trip to hell and back, had lost so many ships and thousands of men to get through to them.

One day in 1944 my father came home very tense and clearly with things on his mind that he could not tell us about. Naturally we did not ask, but equally naturally my mother and I speculated a good deal between ourselves, and kept our eyes open. Once I caught sight of the words Mulberry H — —, the second word being hidden by something else, at the head of a paper among a scatter of others on his bureau. We glanced at each other, and he smiled and deliberately moved it to the bottom of a pile.

The end of his leave came, and he departed, not, on this occasion, to take over another convoy; at least, not the usual kind of convoy. This time his command was the *Sumatra*, the last surviving cruiser of the Dutch Navy, waiting for him at Oban, along with an incredible fleet of outworn and expendable shipping, ripe for the knacker's yard, but still valiant; their last purpose in life, to cross the Channel and sink themselves to form the first breakwaters for the Normandy landings.

The long-awaited Second Front was just about to start. We were going back into Europe.

On 4th June 1944 they sailed. Coasting the Western Highlands, down through the Irish Sea, round Land's End and up the Channel; three days on the trip. The *Sumatra*, well packed with high explosives and all wired up, like the rest of her raggle-taggle fleet, and other fleets of the same kind, all heading in the same direction, to blow her own bottom out at the touch of a switch — or of course at any slight mishap on the way over. It was not, said my father afterwards, a very restful sensation. But he added that he would not have missed the trip for worlds. And never, I think, was any man more proud of the fleet he commanded. At least half of them dropped out and had to be left behind at one time or another, but always they caught up again, belching steam through every rivet-hole, and at the end not one of his lame ducks was missing.

People on the South Coast saw them go by; and saw also the great pale masses of the vast caissons being towed in the same direction, the caissons which formed the second phase of the do-it-yourself breakwaters whose code name was Mulberry Harbour.

They arrived at their appointed beaches, blew their bottoms out and sat down in the mud, at depths carefully calculated to keep their upper warks above water, and the Normandy landings were on. My father's particular beach turned out to be too close under the fire of the German guns and so it was never used, which was sad, though I do not think that it dims the Don Quixote valour of that crazy-comic fleet. And my father came home by destroyer, well laden. Since the Dutch cruiser was certainly going to be looted anyway, he did a little gentle looting himself, and brought back with him a barograph, a vast thick naval blanket with orange stripes at the ends, and the ornamental brass crown off the top of Queen Wilhelmina's portrait photograph in the wardroom.

Then he went back to more orthodox convoys for the duration.

Towards the end of the war, Mike died. Not of old age — though nearly twelve he was still going strong — but of poison. We had always said, with merry laughter, that whatever Mike died of, it would not be poison, for he was a most pernickety eater, and offended many a visitor by refusing titbits with deep and obvious distrust. It was not easy to feed a big Airedale through the war. We had done our best, but a lot of what he got was unsuitable, scrapings off plates, which we could have done with ourselves, and the heels of loaves soaked in gravy; and though I do not think he was ever actually hungry, probably his body was conscious of a lack, just as ours were. And when he found a dead sheep that had been doctored with poison and left for foxes, he made a hearty meal. We knew nothing of what had happened, except that he was not well, and he showed no real signs of poisoning until it was too late for the vet to do anything.

The boy from a nearby farm who occasionally did some gardening for us, our veteran of the leeks and white alyssum having long since retired, dug him a grave alongside Don's, just outside the gate into the wood, and we put his collar on, that he might not run stray and nameless among the stars, and wrapped him in his blanket, like Sir John Moore, and put his beloved blue rubber ball in with him. And when the boy had shovelled back the earth and gone away, and we were left standing over the new grave, my mother read bits of the Burial Service over him, and pushed little wild daffodil bulbs from the bank into the soft earth, ready for the spring. It was Hallowe'en, with a cold grey mist dripping among the trees. And all the while we both cried with quiet desolation, the tears trickling down our noses, for Mike who had come to us at six weeks old and been part of us ever since.

For months afterwards, we heard him about the house, the familiar rattle of his nails on the parquet floor; and often my mother got up and opened the sitting-room door for him, so that he should not feel shut out. Once she said she saw him, lying in front of the hall stove, always a favourite place of his, whether the stove was alight or not. I never saw him, but I wished I had.

Towards the end of the war also, Edward got engaged, though not married until a year later, to a girl in South Africa. His sister Enid, who I suppose must have known how I felt, rang up one lunchtime to tell me before I saw it in the paper, which was kind of her. I can't remember what she said. The thing I remember is that we were having apple-pie for lunch — my father was home on leave, and it was a favourite with him — and after I rang off I went back to my half-empty plate and tried to finish it, and decided I did not really want any more apple-pie, after all. Then I retired to a quiet corner and took off the little silver locket, and put it away in the back of a drawer.

It was quite a long time later that I realised that all my lovely rainbow-coloured dreams of Edward asking me to marry him had always ended in my refusing him with great nobility; a lovely scene of renunciation. And I was forced to admit to myself that I was not really in love with him at all.

I suppose it must have been around the middle of the war that I began to get the itch to write.

As I said before, I took to miniature painting without a completely whole heart, on the advice of my elders and betters. Generally speaking, I do not think that one should ever take another person's advice in the things of life that really matter, but follow the dictates of the still small something in one's innermost self. But 'They' advised, and I bowed to the advice; and in this particular instance it was a good thing I did because the advice turned out to be so resoundingly wrong that it turned me into another direction altogether. If I had gone on working in oils I might very well have been a dedicated but unsuccessful painter to this day. And I do not mean unsuccessful merely in terms of bank balance and public acclaim, but in terms of paint. For as a painter I was too much of a romantic; I would probably have got by all right in a world of Burne-Jones's drop-wristed maidens and knights in armour. But those days were past. Edward said that I needed to paint a string of really ugly and coarse-featured old men. Edward abrogated to himself, in my young days, the rights of a brother, the right to worry about me, the right to hurt me when he thought fit, the right to be utterly foul to me about my painting, and later my writing, while allowing no one else to be so. To some extent he still does. He was right about the ugly old men, but I could not do it. I could not cope with harsh realities in paint; especially I could not cope with them within the small limits of the miniature frame.

Almost from the beginning I felt cramped as a miniature painter and I think my first urge to break out into writing was the result of this. One can write as big as one needs; no canvas is too large to be unmanageable.

So I began to scribble, at first purely for the pleasure of scribbling, and without any idea of getting published. It was a delight, a way of escape, and in early years it had the added attraction of being a forbidden delight, a way of escape that must be kept secret. My family knew that I could paint, but — who shall blame them, remembering my school record — they had no faith whatever in my ability to write. At least, my mother had not. I do not think my father was aware of what I was up to until the war was over, and he returned to be a permanent member of the family again. After that he had no faith either. So my writing, done on sheets of foolscap left over from pre-war Admiralty Sailing Directions, was kept hidden away under the blotting-paper on my painting table or in the back of the big blue airmail pads on which I wrote my weekly letters to my father and Edward. My mother would not have tried to stop me, but she would not have believed in what I was doing. It would have had no validity in her eyes, not at that stage. So I wrote in secret, as many have done before me. I should probably have done so in any case, since of all people in the world, one's family are the people one can least bear to see one's embryo efforts.

And my embryo efforts, looking back on them, were very bad. By Jeffrey Farnol out of Warwick Deeping, combining the worst points of both. How I managed it, considering the literature on which I had been brought up, I cannot imagine. But I did.

Except for a few rather regrettable short stories with a good deal of whimsy about them, the first of my brain children that I can remember was called *Wild Sunrise*, a saga of the Roman invasion of Britain told from the British viewpoint. Its hero, Cradoc, was a young British chieftain, as Victorian-English as anything out of Whyte Melville's *Gladiators*. His adventures went on for ever, because I loved him so much I could not bear to part with him; because, also, I could not think how to bring them to a close. Eventually I did finish the story somehow and stowed it tenderly away in a dark corner. In due course, probably when my father and I moved house after my mother died, it sank without trace, which all things considered is just as well. I should hate, even now, for any eyes but mine to read *Wild Sunrise*, not so much because it was very bad as because so much of me was in it, naked and defenceless. It would be a form of indecent exposure.

Later, not long before the war's end, I produced a story, also long since disappeared, whose loss I do regret. Its name is gone from me, but almost everything else about it I remember as clearly as if I had finished it last week. Like *Wild Sunrise*, it was not written for children, nor yet for adults, but simply for my own delight. And though I have maintained ever since that I cannot write mediaeval because I cannot get inside the mediaeval mind, nor eighteenth-century because anything later than the Civil War turns cloak-and-dagger on me, it was an eighteenth-century story. It is an account of one long summer in the life of a little girl sent to stay with a strict great aunt in Exeter while her mama recovers at Bath from a miscarriage. In the doctor's house next door (he being regarded, as was Dr Hoggins in *Cranford*, as Not Quite a Gentleman), the doctor's ex-soldier son is recovering from wounds received at Minden. The inevitable happens; a hole in the hedge, and the solace of much-needed companionship for a homesick small girl and an embittered young man. Almost the whole summer passes in the garden, a big untidy garden in contrast to

Great Aunt's trim plot, with a mulberry tree in the middle and a few apple trees at the foot. I can see every inch of it now, and catch the dream-rich colours of Provence roses and pinks and crown imperial. Not much happens, except that Great Aunt forbids Jane-Anne's daily visits as being improper, and has to be won over; and the boy has to have his wound re-opened and searched again, at which time Jane-Anne sacrificially destroys the china greyhound, which is her greatest treasure, by dropping it down the well to propitiate the gods. For the most part it was just a study of the developing relationship between the young man and the little girl. In the end it went wrong, because I was too inexperienced to know what I was making, and tried to carry it through to a conventional happy ending years later when Jane-Anne was grown up, not knowing that what I had produced was an idyll, which found its natural end with the summer turning towards autumn, and Jane-Anne's return home, and the young man's departure to walk the wards of a big London hospital on the way to becoming a doctor like his father.

In places it was heavily derivative; I remember a card party in Great Aunt's house, which, with its candles on the table and the enormous shadows of the ladies' mob-caps nid-nodding on the walls behind them, came straight out of *Cranford*. But there were things in it that were good, and that were me, and no one else ... Anyway, it was not really completely lost, because as anyone reading this, who has also read *The Eagle of the Ninth* will have realised, bits and pieces of it, lingering warmly in my mind, found their way, ten or twelve years later, into the summer which Marcus also spends nursing a wound with his Uncle Aquila in Calleva Atrebatum. There is the same basic situation between a Roman soldier with his career broken behind him, and a British girl not so very much older than Jane-Anne; the same need to win over the adult and orthodox world; the boy having his wound re-searched by the Healer with the Knife. But in *The Eagle of the Ninth*, that summer, a 'Kingfisher Summer' as Marcus once thinks of it (Kingfisher Summer would have made a good name for that earlier lost version) is only one part of the story, which leads on to adventure elsewhere; and so I was able to lead it back to the garden eventually, and find as a natural outcome the happy ending which I had failed to find, or at any rate to make convincing, for the story of Jane-Anne.

Not long after the war, I started on a book which I did intend for children, a re-telling of the Celtic and Saxon legends on which my mother had brought me up. Beowulf, Cuchulain, Geraint and Enid, Gawain and the Loathely Lady, about a dozen in all. And writing them, I began for the first time to think about the possibility of getting published, the strange alchemy which would turn a private scribble on foolscap, made for one's own joy in the making, into a book to be opened to the world and read by other people. It seemed that in a sort of way that would be to bring what one had written to birth, and the pregnancy would be just as private and just as much a delight as ever.

When they were finished, I sent the whole collection, copied out in my best long-hand, to my old friend Colonel Crookenden, to see what he thought of them. Why Crooky, I am not sure; I could scarcely have chosen anybody less bookish. But we had always kept in touch. Once, during the war, he had come to see me, rolling up the drive in a jeep, with a wretched young lieutenant whom he bullied unmercifully in attendance, on his way to see the Cheshires, his old regiment, off from somewhere to somewhere else. I was in the habit of writing to him about my more private concerns, and so he seemed the obvious person to send them to.

There are times when life seems to fall into complete patterns, with all the loose ends neatly darned in. It could be chance, or it could be that Fate has a sense of pattern, or it could be God taking an interest. A day or two after receiving my parcel of legends, Crooky chanced to find himself at some social gathering next to the daughter of an old friend, who, born, as it were, into the Cheshire Regiment, had lately married into the Oxford University Press. He told her about the legends and issued his orders, 'I shall send them to you tomorrow, and you will show them to your husband.' I think I have mentioned before that Crooky bore a startling resemblance to Julius Caesar, and possibly for that reason people always found themselves doing what he told them. The stories arrived, the girl did as she was bid. And by and by I received a very kind letter from the Oxford University Press, saying that they didn't want them — which somewhat surprised me since I had known nothing of all that went before.

So, the Oxford University Press did not want my British legends. But the very kind letter went on to suggest that I should try my hand at writing a *Robin Hood* for them.

And that was how it all began.

16

The war was over, the country already heading for the general election which was to turn Mr Churchill out and, for the first time in his life, my father was involved in politics. As a serving officer politics had been out of bounds for him; and in his eight years of retirement he had not been particularly interested. But he liked fair play, and did not hold with kicking a man in the teeth the moment you no longer needed him to sweat his guts out in your service. So on Churchill's behalf, though he did not particularly like him as a man, he sailed into action on the Conservative side, instead of merely voting Conservative when polling day came as he had always done before. And my mother and I were dragged along in his wake.

Yarnscombe Old Vicarage had just been sold to a new owner; a Mrs King with a son just out of the RAF who was suffering from combat fatigue, said local rumours. 'Got to live a quiet life, du'ee see.' Scenting a possible ally or allies, we went to call on them and, in my father's case, enlist their support.

The Vicarage, like the village, was two and a half miles away, and then the best part of another mile down a farm lane. It was a very narrow lane, narrowed still further just then by the growth of high summer; meadowsweet brushing the car on both sides, hazel and cream-curded elder almost joining hands overhead. At last we left the lane to go on by itself and turned in through an ordinary field gate into the Vicarage drive; and so came at last to the typical sprawling many-gabled Victorian Vicarage. On the gravel bay in front of the house a huge and ancient car was standing largely dismantled, and a plump grey-haired woman was standing by, watching whatever it was that the owner of a pair of male legs was doing under the bonnet.

As we appeared, the owner of the legs emerged, and turned round, a tall rangy young man with a typical Aries head crowned by darkly flaming red hair. He had the pinkish skin, even on his big bony hands, that so often and so regrettably goes with hair of that colour (better than the vealy pallor, though, which seems to be almost the only alternative), a moustache which, surprisingly, was not of the woofy RAF variety but more akin to the kind worn by sergeant-majors, a pair of blazingly golden-hazel eyes under thick quirking brows.

There were introductions all round. "This is my son Rupert,' said Mrs King.

And I remember nothing more of that first encounter, and certainly had no idea as we drove home that for me life was never again going to be quite as it had been before.

After that we saw quite a lot of the Kings at political meetings and so forth. A few days after our first call, they came to tea; and when it was time to go home again, standing on the front doorstep, Rupert said, 'Goodbye, Rosemary.'

I was a very old-fashioned girl. I have noticed that the disabled young often are. I suppose it comes of being so much with their elders. And I was so unused to speaking to my own generation anyway, but only to older people, whom one addressed by surname. I said, 'Goodbye, Mr King,' not even thinking about it, certainly not intending a snub. But he said, 'I'm sorry,' and stepped back quickly, with a small odd gesture of one hand, almost as though I had slapped his face.

I did not even know what I had done. Not until he told me, a long while later.

The general election came, and Churchill was out. But we went on seeing quite a lot of the Kings. At all events, I did.

Rupert had got into the way of coming up to collect me and take me down for lunch or tea or supper or all three, to listen to something together on the wireless, or play with Lena the Corgi bitch's new litter of puppies. He was, I think, the first person to whom it ever occurred that I could be asked out without my parents. And more and more, as autumn turned to winter, I enjoyed being down at the Old Vicarage.

And then one wild winter's evening we were sitting by the fire talking, with the old window-shutters fastened to keep out the draughts, and Mrs King off about some concern of her own. Rupert had been talking about flying, as he often did when we were alone; on and on about flying; I think being grounded was a kind of amputation to him at that time, and talking eased the ache in the lost limb. Then, I don't know how, the talk shifted, and he said something about his wife.

I had the most extraordinary sensation. A physical sensation as of being kicked in the stomach by a mule. I remember saying in a small, brittle, 'social' voice, 'How silly of me, I didn't realise you were married.'

And he said, 'Rosemary, I'm sorry, I thought I'd told you.'

I do not believe for a moment that he thought any such thing.

He began to tell me then. It was an all too common story at that time, of a marriage, in his case when he was eighteen, to a woman ten years older than himself, rushed into in case the next raid over Germany might be the last. It had ended in disaster, with two small boys to show for it, and a divorce pending. After he told me, we seemed to be more deeply aware of each other. We seemed to be putting out tendrils. But even then I did not understand the full significance of that sensation of being kicked in the stomach.

On Christmas Eve, both families went to have tea at the Woodford Bridge Hotel. The place was a favourite haunt of

ours (I think it was on that stretch of the river that I had
failed to catch my fish) and despite its rather modern name,
had been an inn for a respectable three or four hundred
years. We were given tea by ourselves in the oak-panelled
room which once had been the taproom, and in which, so
says local tradition, Cromwell spent the night after the
Battle of Torrington. There was a roaring fire, a big bowl
of holly and creamy flower-spikes of chinquerinchee on the
table. Rupert and I left our parents to the fire, and went
and sat on the deep sill in the window embrasure. It must
have been very cold there, but I do not remember that. I
do remember that somebody had given me a big soft green
woollen scarf for Christmas. I had always been superstitious
about wearing green; but it was such a lovely colour, like
moss under oak trees, that greatly daring I had put it on.
Green has been one of my colours ever since. We shared
hot buttered toast from the same plate; and looked at each
other rather a lot. Rupert had a strange trick of the eyes
— Edward has it, too, but I have not seen it in many other
people. A way of looking at you with total concentration; as
it were 'locking in', which some people find disconcerting.

One night at the Old Vicarage that winter, we listened
to Ivor Novello's *Perchance to Dream* on the wireless. It was
only a few years old then, and its small, haunting, fragile
hit-song 'We'll Gather Lilacs' was still a tune that one heard
constantly, on the wireless, from orchestras in restaurants,
being whistled in the street. To this day I have only to hear
the first notes, in some programme of 'Golden Oldies', to
go straight back to that time. What an arid place this world
would be without nostalgia.

> We'll gather lilacs in the Spring again
> And walk together down an English lane
> Until our hearts have learned to sing again
> When you come home once more ...

Rupert was supposed, on doctor's orders, to be living a quiet, outdoor life, working in the garden and things like that. He never did a stroke in the garden if he could avoid it; and his idea of a quiet life was to buy a geriatric sports car tied together with string, and go rocketing round the countryside in it. Throughout the following spring and summer, quite often I went with him. Sometimes, now, someone who does not know my ways will ask if they are driving too fast for me. They do not know that I was once in the habit of being driven at eighty — not that that is any great speed now, I know — in a car with a cocoa-tin lid tied over the oil-filter, and a piece of rope leading across my chest from one door-handle to the other, as the only means of keeping the doors shut.

Sometimes he would bring the family car instead, because of its higher clearance, and we would wander down deeply rutted lanes and farm tracks, or even drive straight across country as though the old lady were a Land Rover. Sometimes it rained, and we would have 'car picnics', with the droplets trickling down the windscreen, and sit talking and holding hands. Occasionally, and gently undemanding of each other, we kissed.

Once he took me to the pictures. It was Roger Livesey and Wendy Hiller in *I Know Where I'm Going*. But mostly we just wandered round the country. We saw a kingfisher blue-flashing upriver on the tawny reed-rustling fringe of Fremington Marshes, read *Hassan* to each other at the top of Dark Ham woods. On the afternoon beyond all afternoons — it must have been fairly early summer, because the elder blossom was heavy and rank-sweet scented over the whole countryside — we came upon the mouth of a tiny lane turned almost into a tunnel by the hazel bushes arching over it. We were almost past before we saw it, and Rupert said, 'Ha! The Golden Road to Samarkand!' and swung the nose

of the car round into it at the last instant. Mercifully there
was nothing on our tail at the time. And we went on and on,
the grass-grown lane leading us, and we following, dazzled
by the dapple of sun through the nut leaves overhead, and
came out at the gate of a little secret meadow sloping down
to the Torridge. Elder-flowers drooped over the gateway;
the riverbank was afroth with pink and white balsams; and
Rupert found a tiny emerald frog in the grass, and caught it
to show me, just for a moment, sitting on his thumb, then let
it go again. We had thermos-flask tea, and talked, holding
hands, and shared the water-sounds and the elder-scent of
the little secret meadow; and nothing else happened, all
the long sunshiny, shadow-dappled afternoon. But if it was
given me to live over again one afternoon of my life, that
would be the one that I should choose.

The odd thing is that neither of us thought of what was
happening to us as Falling in Love. We thought that it was
something different and special. Everybody in love thinks
that their love is special, an experience which nobody else
has had before. But we did not think of it as being in love
at all, only as being two halves of the same thing. From the
first we had a strong sense of relationship, though in the
early days it might as well have been a sibling relationship as
any other. In those days we both believed in reincarnation,
as I rather think I still do, so we tried to rationalise the
thing as a link formed in other lives. Perhaps we had been
brothers, sisters, lovers, comrades in arms. 'There is only
one love,' Rupert said, trying to work it out as he went along.
'All the different kinds of love are just facets of it.'

Even when he asked me one day, if when he was married
to 'some incredibly beautiful wife', I would come and make
a third in the household, I was not shocked or unhappy or
furious; not at that stage. I had already accepted that he was
not monogamous by nature, that he was quite incapable of

finding all he wanted in one woman, and would always go wandering in search of the missing parts, but that he could probably be perfectly faithful to two or three. If he had been a Muslim and allowed three wives, I should have been one of them within the next year or so; and probably the favourite one at that. How could I understand all this, and yet not really understand that we were quite simply in love but face to face with problems that we could not handle? Perhaps it was a kind of protective barrier put up by both of us because the problems were insoluble, lying as they did both in ourselves and in our surrounding world.

My father was in strong opposition from the beginning. His Puritan streak did not want a divorced man, let alone one who was not yet even properly divorced, anywhere around his daughter. Also he loved me and didn't want me hurt. What was worse, he didn't even understand that I had the right to be hurt. 'Take what you want,' saith the Lord, 'take it and pay for it.' And the bleak disapproval that met us at the door every time Rupert brought me home would have rubbed out all the shiningness of the time that we had spent together, if anything could have done that. My mother thought that it was just Edward over again, and would dissipate itself harmlessly in due course, and was happy for me that meanwhile I was getting something in return for what I gave, this time. Rupert's mother never understood a thing, not a thing, at any rate with regard to Rupert's feelings. To her it would have been so unnatural, so unthinkable that her son could fall in love with a girl with my physical disability, that she never saw the thing at all. Once, Rupert said to me, 'I bet Mother's told you I call all girls darling. But there are darlings and darlings.' And she had. But she had told me for my sake, not for Rupert's.

The mixture of opposition with a general consensus of opinion that nothing between us existed for real, because nothing could, coloured our own attitude to what was happening to us. And we were so young. Oh, twenty-four is an age of discretion, but we were so young for our age, even the half of us who had fathered two children and spent the last three years as a bomber pilot. So young and vulnerable to the pressure of other people's attitudes.

In the years since then there has been a gradual change in the climate of ideas with regard to the disabled. It has begun to dawn on the able-bodied world that it is possible to combine an unsatisfactory body with a perfectly satisfactory brain, and a personality at any rate as satisfactory as most other people's. Trailing somewhat behind that, but now beginning to emerge also, is the much more startling idea that the disabled may not only have normal brains and the ability to hold down normal jobs and the wish to join in normal recreations and be accepted for ourselves, just as people, but normal emotions also. That we may have the same emotional needs as anybody else, and the ability to satisfy those needs in each other, or even in the able-bodied.

It is an idea that still seems faintly shocking, or sentimentally sweet but quite impractical, or just plain inconceivable, to some people. But the change in attitude is beginning. I have often wondered, if it had begun thirty years ago, whether it would have made any difference to Rupert and me.

As it was, we simply couldn't cope. We never really brought our feelings out into the open, or admitted the situation to each other. Rupert might have said, 'I love you, but if we get married, I shan't be faithful to you. I know me. I haven't got what it takes to be married to a woman with your handicaps, and I should begin to take it out on you.' And I might have said, 'I love you, and I'm ready to risk that.' And Rupert would have said, 'But I'm not.' So it probably wouldn't have made any difference in the long run. But it would have been better for us both, none the less, if we could have faced and shared our predicament in some such way. Better at the time, and better to remember afterwards.

We came to summer's end; and Mrs King sold the Old Vicarage and went to live in Dorset; and Rupert went off to a job in London. We parted with, of all unlikely things, an exchange of little boxes by way of keepsakes; mine to him, a little box of inlaid wood that I had kept my more minuscule treasures in since I was a child; his to me, a small casket of brass and copper and silver arabesques lined with cedarwood, in which he had kept his collar-studs, and in which I keep my paper-clips to this day. And I settled down to work, harder even than I had been working before, at my painting, and at researching and note-taking and rough-draughting my *Robin Hood*. Work hard enough, and I might not notice how the days were drawing in, and how lonely the wind sounded at night.

Rupert was no letter writer, but we wrote to each other every three or four days, all that winter. I dreamed of him a lot. We tried deliberately to dream of each other, to see if it was possible for two people as close as we were to share the same dreams. But as far as I know, we never succeeded in that.

Just after Christmas, he came down and collected me, in the face of my father's iron disapproval — I was used to the sensation of a black pall hanging over the house that was produced by my poor mother's depressions, but before Rupert appeared on the scene I had never experienced the dun-coloured fog that expressed my father's disapproval — and took me off to spend a few days with his mother in her adorable little golden stone cottage in Beaminster.

Daniel's Cottage, Shadrack Street. It sounds like something out of a story book. The steep and narrow cottage staircase was impossible for me, and I slept on a put-you-up in a little room off the kitchen, whose small high window looked up over the top of the high garden wall to the wavering tawny shingle roof and fairytale chimneys of the cottage opposite, where pigeons strutted and crooned, displaying the green and purple iridescence of their necks.

Again we wandered the countryside in Rupert's car; to Bridport and Cerne, and along the coast to Abbotsbury in search of swans. There were more evenings by the fire, while Rupert strung up on green silk the beads of an old broken Venetian glass necklace that he had found for me in a junk shop.

One day he took me off to a very fine physiotherapist who had his surgery in the little town, a St Dunstan's man, blinded in the First World War. It was arranged, when he took me home, that I should come back in a week or so, and lodge with Mrs King, and have a month's course of treatment.

It did not work out quite as planned. That was the New Year of 1947 and, within a few days, one of the famous winters of this century had clamped down on us.

'More snow with considerable drifting is forecast for all districts of the British Isles except the South West,' said the weather forecast day after day with wearisome monotony. And we would look out at the white waste beyond the windows, the snow drifted to the sills, and wonder how much further south-west was south-west. For two months we were almost entirely cut off. From time to time my father walked into Torrington along the tops of the hedges, with a knapsack on his back, to do the more desperately urgent shopping. We were all right for milk, which came from a nearby farm. The postman got through to us once in ten days or a fortnight; and for me there would be a handful of longed-for letters from Rupert before the silence and the waiting settled down again. Sometimes in the middle of the day when the sun was out there would come tiny green trickling sounds, a few bright drops falling reluctantly from the tips of icicles, holding out false hopes of a thaw. But always, the moment the sun was gone, the freeze clamped down again like iron. It seemed as though the world was dead and would never warm back to life again. The spring would never come, and my month in Beaminster with Rupert coming down at weekends. It had all gone far away into a kind of unreality. I could not talk about it, even to my mother, who, finding I suppose, that the thing was more serious than she had thought, was going over more and more to my father's point of view.

The weeks dragged on, through February and far into March. Just before the end, as a grand finale, we had a fog, causing a silver frost. I have never known anything more beautiful and enchanted and terrible than our wood in the murderous grip of that silver frost. Every branch, every twig was sheathed in many times its own thickness of clear ice. When the wind blew, the branches rang against each other making a cold-sweet music as of glass bells, while after dark, under a full moon, the wood was full of shifting points of light, as though whole constellations of stars had fallen out of the frosty sky to become entangled in those strange ghost-pale branches. It was Hans Andersen, a Snow Queen's Kingdom with splinters of death at its heart.

When, soon after, the thaw came at last, and the strange enchantment fell away, the heart was laid bare. Great branches torn away by the weight of ice and hanging by a few ragged filaments of wood or bark, like human limbs half blown off in some horrible disaster; hardly any of the big trees had escaped without mutilation of some kind. And my father, who was a first-rate woodsman, was appalled, on one level at the amount of work to be done, and on another by the amount of wreckage that was for all time and could never be set right.

Spring came quickly after the thaw, celandines starring

the ditches almost before the snowdrops were out, catkins dancing on the torn hazel sprays, the whole world urgent with bursting buds as though trying to catch up with lost time. But it was a long time before the season got itself sorted out. It must have been the very end of March when I went back to Beaminster; but the narrow high-walled garden of Daniel's Cottage was flickering with the coloured flame points of crocuses, white and purple and lilac and gold, and each crocus opening to the sunlight seemed to me at once a star and a grail; a cup brimming with light. It is one of the Mysteries, surely, this sense of light shining through rather than on; the whole world become faintly translucent and the light of the spirit shining through its substance, that comes with being in love. One has it as a child, but in childhood one knows nothing else and so is not conscious of it, until the heightened awareness is given back for this one time. Maybe it is akin to some kind of spiritual awareness. Maybe saints feel like that all the time. I know that all the past summer and now again, I was so happy that I felt also holy. I had one less skin between me and the universe. I felt an incredible kindness towards all the world; a desire to take its sorrows on my shoulders, because that would be only fair.

Rupert did not come down the first weekend. On the next, he was due on the Friday evening, But suddenly in the middle of that day I was filled with the most appalling sense of loss, of bereavement. My first thought was of my mother and father. They had gone away on a short motoring holiday. Could there have been a car crash? As the day went on, I knew that it was not them. I did not know who or what it was, but the sense of loss, the fear and desolation persisted. When Rupert arrived safe and sound in the evening, I was almost sick with relief. But still, the feeling did not quite go away. And Rupert, though he was as affectionate as ever, more so if anything, seemed not quite the Rupert I knew.

But he was always moody, and I told myself, and almost made myself believe, that it was just one of his moods.

He came and kissed me goodnight after I was in bed. He sat for a long time on the edge of the little cramped put-you-up, just touching the blister on my shoulder where the electrical treatment I was receiving had been over-enthusiastic. But I knew that something was wrong, and I did not sleep that night.

Next morning he asked me to come and have coffee with him in the small genteel teashop nearby. And there he told me — asking me not to tell anybody else, even his mother, especially his mother, because the divorce was not yet absolute — that he had met a girl called Gilli, and they were going to get married as and when they could. She and I must meet, we must become friends, very close to each other. 'A threefold cord is not easily broken,' he quoted over and over again.

'A threefold cord is not easily broken,' I agreed, doing my best for him; knowing now the meaning of my appalling sense of loss. I was halfway through a small lemon cake with yellow icing and mimosa-balls on it. It is odd that my worst moments should remain in my mind indelibly connected with food. It is undignified and it is unjust, because I have never been very food orientated. I managed to finish it as though it had not turned to sickly sawdust.

Last summer I had been able to accept that Rupert was not monogamous, and no one woman would ever satisfy all of him. I had accepted that in a society that allowed him two or three wives I would have been one, but I could not be the only one. But last summer, that had been a thing to do with the future; and while the world shone from within with that clear beauty, the future was safely away out of touch. Now, the future was here, and we did not live in a Muslim society, for all Rupert's talk of threefold cords.

I finished my sickly cake, and we went back to Daniel's Cottage, and the light had gone out of the crocuses.

I got through the rest of that month somehow, and my family collected me. My mother was bitterly disappointed that the course of physiotherapy had not had more dramatic results than it had. She said I looked very white; and what had I been doing to get those spots? She had never known me to have spots before.

I said it must have been the porridge Mrs King liked for supper. I seemed to have heard at some time that porridge had given me spots when I was two. So why not now?

17

I had not been home more than a week when Rupert wrote asking me if I could and would come up to London for a few days. He had all arrangements made for me to stay with an old friend of his mother's who kept a small private hotel in Thurlow Square. He could get four days off from his job. Margot Fonteyn was dancing in *The Sleeping Beauty* at Covent Garden; the Lady of the Unicorn tapestries were on exhibition at the V and A, the lilac would be out at Kew, and I must meet Gilli.

I suppose that if this was somebody else's story it would seem to me almost incredible that the girl even considered going. Had she no proper pride, I would wonder. But it is my story, and the truth is that where Rupert was concerned, it was 'Whistle and I'll come to you, my lad'. I had no pride, proper or otherwise, and never felt the need of any. What I felt for him made pride seem a kind of excess baggage, and certainly not to be confused with self-respect.

Also there was this thing about the threefold cord. And if it was true, as I still think it probably is, that there is only one love, and all the specialized loves are merely facets of it …

What does seem to me almost incredible is that I ever found the courage to tell my father that I was going to London for four days to stay with a friend of Mrs King's and spend my time with Rupert.

I went to London by train, my father having tipped the guard to keep an eye on me and see that I was all right. To his everlasting credit be it said that, hating the whole idea as he did, and without relaxing or attempting to hide one iota of his disapproval, he never attempted to stop me from going. Neither did my mother; but she was still a little on my side after all, still wanted me to have whatever of happiness I could, and at times even half-accepted my right to live life and be hurt by it, just for a little while. I wonder what their reactions would have been if I had been free to tell them about Gilli. I really do wonder. Would they have thought that if I could even think of going off for those four days with a new girl-friend already on the scene, then the thing must be cooling off after all and there could not be much to worry about? Or would they have felt that her existence made the whole plan humiliating and intolerable? I don't know.

It was not humiliating or intolerable. When we met, we quite liked each other. At least, I quite liked Gilli. What she felt about me, I have no means of knowing; she was extremely nice to me; she must have known that she had to be, for she was no fool. But we only met a couple of times, and it is surprising how small a part she plays in my memory of those four days. They say, of course, that you forget the things you do not want to remember.

Rupert met me at Waterloo, with a new car; that is to say, a car that was not the old one of last summer's picnics, but just as geriatric and just as tied up with string. He took me to dinner at some small atmospheric place with red banquettes to sit on; and my four days, which were most likely going to have to last me a lifetime, had begun. The red banquette swayed gently under me with the movement of the train, for I was very tired, and with more than the journey. We held hands, and looked at one another, like John Betjeman's couple in the teashop inglenook, and for once I do not remember what we ate. We were happy, sharing a kind of peace at being together again. It seems strange that I could be so happy. It was a broken-winged happiness that could not fly any more, but it was there, all the same, and it lasted, as the precious four days went by.

We went to the Zoo. Rupert always had a boy's passion for the Zoo. And there he took me to see Chi Chi the Giant Panda. She had climbed to the top of her cage and was crouching among the roof girders as though to get as far away from people as possible. She looked clotted with misery, as sad a sight in her way as the squirrel in its cage in Poole Park, though this time, having learned to conform, I did not have to be removed howling. When she died, not so long after, I was not surprised, and not sorry, since there was no other way to freedom for her.

We went to spend an enchanted morning among the Lady of the Unicorn tapestries at the Victoria and Albert, delighting in the Lady of each tapestry, in her high winged or steeple-crowned headdress, her skirts trailing through the minuscule world of rabbits and heartsease pansies and pinks and little birds with which her creator had lovingly filled every square inch of each rose-red background. And she playing on small gilded organs or posing elegantly between formal long-stemmed trees or in the looped-back entrance of tasselled pavilions; always with her attendant leafy-tailed unicorn and sometimes a lion as well.

We went to Kew; into the Gardens through what I have always thought of as the Unicorn gate, now closed, and looked up in the first moment of entering to see on a small steep mound to our left a tiny mock-classical temple arched over by a magnolia tree. The lilac was not yet in its full flush, but the late magnolias were everywhere, some still perfect, some beginning to shed faintly brown-tipped petals at every stirring of the little wind. I remember being in the heart of a whole thicket of magnolias, the pale waxen flowers seeming to float on the scented air all round my head, as water-lilies float on the surface of a pool, and underfoot the fallen petals that gave off a paean of scent as one stepped on them. And everywhere the booming of the bees. We had lunch in the shadow of the Pagoda, and afterwards sat on the grass under a lime tree not yet broken into leaf. Rupert lay with his head on his arm, turned towards me, holding my wrist in his free hand. People came and went along the path nearby. It didn't matter. The sun through the branches made a kind of shadow-net that lay across us both.

On three of our four nights we went to Covent Garden. All three of us to see Moira Shearer with her flame-red hair dance *Les Sylphides* among a couple of other short ballets. Just Rupert and me to *The Sleeping Beauty*; and on the third night to the first opera of my life, *The Magic Flute*, the famous production in which Sarastro made his first entrance in a chariot drawn by lions, and Tamino wore a rather regrettable helmet that looked for all the world like a vast golden harebell. The powers who plan such things could have done no better if they had planned the whole season to provide those three magical evenings for Rupert and me.

On the fourth night, which was Sunday and wet, it was the three of us again, car-wandering round Dockland — oh, the wet-black-shining of the rainy streets in the light of the street lamps! — and joining some other friends of Rupert's for a dinner of strange and unfathomable things in a vast array of little bowls, among bamboo screens and fragile paper lanterns in a Chinese restaurant.

There were the odd times in Rupert's one-roomed flat, too, when an hour's quiet and a mug of Café-Polonaise, which was a speciality of his, seemed like a good idea. Once, there was a strong smell of onions coming in through the open window, and I remarked on it. 'That will be the Were Leopard,' said Rupert over the gas-ring. 'Were Leopards' breath always smells of onions.'

'What would be the thing to do, if a Were Leopard came in over the window sill?' I wondered, with some interest.

'Make it comfortable in the best armchair, give it a cigar, and then beetle downstairs and phone the fire brigade,' said Rupert.

One of the good things about being with Rupert was that we not only 'made music together' to use a phrase that had not then been coined, we also made nonsense. There was the time we stood together gazing into a starkly empty shop window in Bridport High Street, and I said, 'I rather like that one in the corner.'

'The green one or the yellow one?'

'The pink one with white spots and the twiddly bit on top.'

Rupert instantly and cordially agreed. 'That kind are the best really. We had one for years when I was a boy. It lived up the chimney, but we couldn't cure it of eating the goldfish.'

Instant lunacy is a pleasure that I have never been able to share to such an extent with anybody before Rupert, or anybody since. It remains part of my more cherished memories, something that I would not have missed for all the clockwork oranges in Lombard Street.

So the four days passed, and were over.

The plan was for Rupert to drive me down to my Uncle Harold's at Poole, and for my mother and father to meet us there and spend the night before the three of us went home. But just short of Winchester an ominous banging from somewhere deep in the bowels of the ancient car told us that the big-end had gone. In Rupert's and my affairs there was so often an inconclusiveness, a sort of black comedy. If we had been Romeo and Juliet, the balcony would undoubtedly have collapsed. We staggered into Winchester banging like a steel band, stabled the car, phoned that we should be late, and continued the journey ignominiously by train.

Watching the Dorset countryside, white with hawthorn, slide past the train window, I felt robbed. Even the last hour that we would have been alone together had now to be got through in a railway carriage full of other people.

The train pulled in to Poole Station, and there on the platform was a reception committee of my father and mother and Uncle Harold.

Rupert came back to the house for tea, but the invitation was not very pressing and the welcome not very warm. And he soon left to catch the next train back to London.

Why does it seem so much more final when somebody goes away in a train than when they drive off in a car?

My mother expected me to chat all evening, giving them all a full account of the past four days. I did my best. I knew also that it was time to make casual mention of a girl called Gilli, whom I had met among some friends of Rupert's, otherwise, when she became as it were public property, I should have to pretend that I had not met her, which might give rise to complications later on. Questions of why I had met her and not mentioned it.

Soon after the divorce went through, and Gilli did become public property. I was already under sore pressure from the family. My father never said anything, now; not to me. But his silence was the silence of estrangement, deeply hurting to us both. My mother had finally decided that enough was enough. She did not actually join forces with my father, in fact I think that to him she tried to take my part; but to me she kept on and on and on, telling me how foolish I was being, and how unhappy I was making them both by refusing to break all links with Rupert.

Rupert was getting married. Rupert sent me a book. It was only Joan Grant's latest novel; he and I were both keen readers of her books at that time. That was the final straw. My father, still with a bleak unhappy face, said nothing. My mother did all the talking. Of course I must send the book back, I must, must, must break with Rupert completely.

No use protesting, as I did protest, that Rupert and I were friends and one did not break with one's friends because they got married. She understood too much of the truth to be bought off by that. In the end she cried and told me that she could not desert me, and so, because of her efforts to take my part, I was tearing a gulf between her and my father.

I don't know how true it was, I only know that I could not take any more.

I sent back the book. I wrote to Rupert explaining the whole sorry situation. In a vacuum we might have managed some kind of threefold relationship. In a world full of other people, it could not be done. At least by me.

Then I had a reconciliation with my father. I sat on his knee like a little girl again, his arms round me; even wept a few difficult tears on his Harris tweed shoulder. It was so lovely not to have that silent barrier of ice between us any more. Such a relief to lay down my weapons, not that I had ever had many weapons — only my little wooden sword — and stop fighting. For the moment it almost outweighed all the rest.

Rupert wrote me a last parting letter, accepting my decision — only it was not a decision, just a capitulation to circumstances too strong for me — but insisting, 'This isn't the end, even this time round, it isn't the end, for you and me.'

He was right, too, though except for one very glancing encounter, it was more than twenty years before I saw him again. 'But that,' as Kipling would have said, 'is another story.'

Edward, the one person I had taken fully into my confidence, was worried on my behalf; not, I think, afraid of my being hurt, but afraid that the hurt would embitter the rest of life for me.

I had always known that that was a completely groundless fear, and now that the hurt had come, I knew it still. Because of what had happened between Rupert and me, I was a fuller and richer person than I would otherwise have been. I knew that if a pantomime fairy in a gauze ballet skirt had appeared, and offered, with one wave of her tinsel wand, to wipe out the last two years, and with them the grey ache of loss that they had left behind, I would not for one moment have considered accepting her offer. Because of those two years, something in me which, without them, would probably have remained green and unawakened, had had a chance to flower and fruit and ripen. Because of those two years I was going, in some odd way, to be able to write as I would not otherwise have been able to do.

I had finished *The Chronicles of Robin Hood* by that time, and sent it to a typing agency, where I think it must have been lost, because it was eighteen months and a great many letters later that it returned to me. In the interval I set to work again, and the result was *The Queen Elizabeth Story*. The QES was a book for little girls, too cosy and too sweet, as were the next two or three books to follow it, before I found, as it were, my own voice. But it was a real book, whereas *Robin Hood* was a foster-child, it was my own, bone of my bone, flesh of my flesh, as *Wild Sunrise* and the nameless idyll about Jane-Anne had been, but reasonably well handled, and carried through to its proper end. Because of what had happened inside me, out of the hurt and the increase, I had made the transition from the amateur, dreaming and scribbling, to the writer, however much at the apprentice stage.

I did not have to write in secret any more. But it had to be kept very clearly for my spare time; the time when I would not, in any case, have been painting miniatures; for my family's faith in me as a writer was still small. That is not to be wondered at, seeing that all I had to show for my efforts at that stage was the rejection of one book of re-told legends, and a request to try my hand at a *Robin Hood* which was now lost and might or might not be any good if ever it were found again.

So *The Queen Elizabeth Story* was finished and sent off to the Oxford University Press, and after a long wait, a letter arrived with 'Oxford University Press' printed on the envelope. I looked at it, feeling sick. Did the fact that it was a letter, just a letter and not a parcel, mean anything? Was the rejected manuscript following under separate cover? Finally, in sudden frantic haste, I butchered the envelope open and tore out the letter. *The Queen Elizabeth Story* was accepted! There was something at the bottom about a £50 advance on royalties. I came back to that part later, for the moment all that mattered was the acceptance. It had been written with so much of delight, and, as many first books are, without the effort and the birth pangs that later one comes to know. It had been written out of heartache, but also out of something set free within myself. And now it was going to be born into the world. It was going to be a book. I had a strong sense of morning and springtime. I must have been much more resilient in those days than I am now.

My mother had another wonderful time being humble!

My father made no attempt to be humble at all. If he had not been such a quiet man, I would have said that he crowed.

In old age he invented a joke. 'Once, Rosemary Sutcliff used to be my daughter; but I'm Rosemary Sutcliff's father now.'

I said to him, 'Darling, do be careful who you say that to.' But he never learned. He said it happily to all the wrong people; and then it would be for me to try to disabuse their minds of the idea that he was jealous.

Soon after *The Queen Elizabeth Story* was accepted, my wandering *Robin Hood* returned to me, and both books were eventually published in the same year.

Soon after, also, I began to keep a diary. But of the years before the diary, all the years since the stork mistook our front door for Mrs McPhee's, this is the only record.

Notes on the text

BY KATE MACDONALD

1

Coopers Hill: the Royal Indian Engineering College based at Cooper's Hill, Egham, in Surrey, trained civil engineers for work in India in the government's Public Works department until 1906.

Epsom and St Thomas's: Epsom College was founded as a Victorian boarding school for the sons of impoverished of deceased medical practitioners; St Thomas's is still one of the great teaching hospitals in London.

Conway, **Dartmouth**: HMS *Conway* was a Royal Navy school training ship for boys who could or did not want to take the naval academy training for officers offered at the Britannia Royal Naval College at Dartmouth, Devon.

pass out: complete his school training.

King's binoculars: Queen Victoria instituted the prize of an inscribed binocular glass to HMS *Conway* students competing for cadetships in the Royal Navy. George Sutcliff would have been awarded his binoculars by Edward VII.

2

Dr Still: George Frederic Still (1868-1941) was a British paediatrician and a leader in identifying childhood illnesses. He was the first to name juvenile idiopathic or rheumatoid arthritis, which Sutcliff suffered from.

Beaver: a game played by schoolboys in a period when beards had become unfashionable, of awarding points for every beard seen in the street in a set time.

Malta fever: brucellosis, an infectious illness caused by drinking unpasteurised milk.

3

Tooting Bec: a district of south-west London.

Children's Hour: a daily BBC radio programme for children, with stories and talks, beginning the history of broadcasting for children's entertainment as opposed to education.

4

The Secret Garden: the novel by Frances Hodgson Burnett (1911), in which a high-walled garden is rediscovered by the children, supported grudgingly by an elderly estate gardener.

London Pride: a small white saxifrage that grows freely in most soils, with five pinkish-white petals on each flowerhead.

saltings: areas of saltwater marsh where the land is flooded regularly by tides.

coxs'n: abbreviation for coxswain, the sailor in charge of the boat, under the officer in charge of the expedition.

This is Your Life: long-running British television programme which featured a surprise presentation of their life to a celebrity or distinguished person, with appearances by significant people from their past, whom they might not have seen for decades.

Oh, poop poop!: quotation from Kenneth Grahame's *The Wind In The Willows*, from the Toad's joyful discovery of the possibilities of a motor car, indicating extreme and perfect bliss.

Fight the Good Fight: a Victorian hymn.

5

'The Knife and the Naked Chalk': from Rudyard Kipling's collection *Rewards and Fairies* (1910).

on appro: tradesman's abbreviation for 'on approval', when goods were sent to the house to be considered and paid for, or sent back.

pice: an Indian unit of currency, worth very little.

tipped: the old custom of gentlemen tipping small children in their family whom they were visiting, or being visited by, quite often with more than the weekly pocket-money.

6

lamp-smitch: the sticky oily residue left after burning.

7

hundreds-and-thousands: the British name for sugar strands, coloured fragments of sugar thread mainly used now for decorating cakes and trifle.

Crummles: a theatrical family in Charles Dickens' novel *Nicholas Nickleby*.

The Little Match-Girl: a story by Hans Christian Andersen, which has a deeply affecting ending.

Peer Gynt: a very popular verse-play by Henrik Ibsen (1867) with incidental music by Edvard Grieg, which combines Norwegian folklore with satire and surreal elements.

8

Queen Mary's Dolls' House: a substantial doll's house built between 1921 and 1924 for Queen Mary, as a celebration of British art and design for the home. It was on display to the public at the Empire Exhibition in Wembley for seven months from July 1924, and then moved to a special room in Windsor Castle, still visited today.

Traitor's Gate: the entrance to the Tower of London on the Thames where those condemned of treason were brought by water to prison, and eventual execution.

Crufts: the leading British dog show, where dogs of breeds are judged for different characteristics. Best Dog is the overall prize winner.

Cranford: a short and very popular novel about the lives of a trio of ladies in a Victorian county town by Elizabeth Gaskell (1853).

Quality Street: a popular 1901 play by J M Barrie about two ladies who open a school for 'genteel' children.

The Cuckoo Clock: a children's fantasy novel by Mrs Molesworth (1877).

Slaves of the Lamp: from two episodes in Kipling's novel *Stalky & Co* (1899), the name for former pupils of the school which formed their characters and determined the courses of their careers.

9

Angela Brazil: the most famous British author of stories for girls in the early decades of the twentieth century, mainly set in boarding schools.

The Schoolgirl's Own: a British weekly story magazine for girls, set in a school. It ran from 1921 to 1936.

the IVth: the British school system arranged children by year group in 'forms', with a lower and an upper form for each number, through which children proceeded as they advanced through the school. The Fourth Form in girls' school stories was traditionally the time when fourteen- and fifteen-year old girls are at their most lively and inventive and also untrammelled by the need to work for important exams.

the last steps of Caesar's throne: a metaphor for the ultimate authority and dispenser of justice.

Sir Christopher Cradock: After receiving ambiguous orders from the Admiralty the naval officer Sir Christopher Cradock (1862–1914) initiated the Battle of Coronel off the coast of Chile against the overwhelming force of the German navy. He died with 1,660 of his men, in the first defeat of the British navy in a hundred years.

11

bridge coat: a short loose jacket worn over an evening dress or day dress as an extra layer when sitting still to play bridge in indifferently heated houses.

quarterings: his family had had their own coats of arms going back at least three generations.

PNEU: Parents' National Educational Union, a British educational organisation founded in 1887.

Oak Apple Day: formerly a public holiday in England, Ireland and Wales to commemorate the restoration of the Stuarts to the monarchy.

12

Toc H: the acronym for Talbot House, an international Christian movement formed during the First World War that serves by providing clubs and day centres, and hospital visits.

Rotary: Rotary Clubs are local business associations that raise funds for local charities and offer services for local people.

Jack Cornwell Medal: Jack Cornwell was a 16 year old English sailor who died from wounds received while serving at his post on HMS *Chester* in 1916, under attack during the Battle of Jutland. He was awarded a posthumous Victoria Cross for devotion to duty as such a young age. The Scouts' Association created the Cornwell Scout Badge in his memory, awarded to Scouts for character, devotion to duty, courage and endurance.

that annoying Spartan youth: the story of the Spartan youth reflects on Spartan culture valuing hardihood and obedience to orders above all others. The Spartan youth disobeyed his tutor by picking up the fox to take home, and then endured the fox gnawing at his flesh because he did not want to be found out.

witchball green: a medieval English custom of hanging out spheres of green blown glass in cottage windows to prevent witches from entering.

13

Mrs Patrick Campbell: one of the great English Edwardian stage actresses.

Rose of Tralee: the subject of the Victorian Irish ballad of the same name, celebrated for her beauty and streadfastness.

14

ITMA* and *Happidrome: *ITMA* was the popular acronym for *It's That Man Again*, a popular radio comedy show on the BBC. *Happidrome* was a radio variety show about a theatre that functioned as a vehicle for guest stars from real-life stage and screen.

Dad's Army: the nickname for the Home Guard, a civil defence force made up of men too old and too young to join the armed forces.

lights: animal lungs, rarely used in British cookery.

library books: bookshops often carried a small stock of new books that would be lent out to customers with a subscription, as an alternative to municipal free libraries.

Gerard's *Herbal:* an antiquarian treasure, a famous seventeenth-century book on plants.

15

Sir John Moore: commander of the British forces on the Iberian Peninsula at the Battle of Corunna during the Peninsular Wars against Napoleon. He was buried wrapped in his military cloak after dying of his wounds from the battle.

Burne-Jones: Sir Edward Burne-Jones, one of the English Pre-Raphaelite painters whose figures invariably had them drooping at the wrist or neck.

By Jeffrey Farnol out of Warwick Deeping: using animal-breeding phrasing Sutcliff is saying that her earliest writing was as bad as if it had been jointly produced by Farnol, an Edwardian novelist who specialised in best-selling historical romance, with the tortured social dynamics of Warwick Deeping.

Whyte Melville's *Gladiators*: the Scottish Victorian novelist George Whyte-Melville was the author of the historical novel *The Gladiators* (1863), among many others.

Minden: a battle in the Seven Years War, fought in 1759 between the British and German armies against the French.

Hassan: a widely anthologised and quoted verse-drama from 1913 by James Elroy Flecker, subtitled *The Golden Journey to Samarkand.*

St Dunstan's man: St Dunstan's was a pioneering rehabilitation hospital for the blind and partially sighted, founded in the First World War.

three-fold cord: from Ecclesiastes 4.12, meaning that three people can withstand great pressure more strongly than only two.

17

Margot Fonteyn: at this date Fonteyn had just been made a prima ballerina with the Royal Ballet and her leading role in *The Sleeping Beauty* was one of her signature roles.

the Lady of the Unicorn tapestries: this set of six fifteenth-century tapestries depicting an extended allegory of the five senses are owned now by the Musée de Cluny, Paris, and would have been on temporary loan to the Victoria and Albert Museum.

John Betjeman's couple: from John Betjeman's poem 'In a Bath teashop' (1945).

> 'Let us not speak, for the love we bear one another –
> Let us hold hands and look.'
> She, such a very ordinary little woman;
> He, such a thumping crook;
> But both, for a moment, little lower than the angels
> In the teashop's ingle-nook.'